Pra

"As a retired L... ....mily law mediator, who has handled literally hundreds of cases involving the sale of the family residence, I know that next to custodial issues with children, no other issue in divorce is fraught with as much tension, misunderstanding, and anger as the sale of the family residence. This book is a must read for all attorneys handling family home sales and should be given to all family law litigants."

—**Hon. MARTHA E. BELLINGER,** judge retired, author of *From Robe to Robe*

"Laurel Starks has written an informative book on a subject that often gets ignored—until it hits hard: selling the family home in a divorce. In her book *Divorcing the House*, she does a complete walk-through of the unique issues involved in selling a house at one of the worst times in a person's life, including: whether to sell, how to deal with the kids, the mortgage, a high-conflict divorce, the proceeds of sale (if any), on up to what a judge might do in court. Yet she recognizes the emotional elements and adds a lot of personal encouraging comments. It's also sprinkled with dozens of examples from her wide experience with many upset couples as a real estate agent specializing in divorce home sales. This book has been needed for quite a while. It will fill a gap for spouses who feel overwhelmed and in need of clear and simple advice from an expert who understands."

—**BILL EDDY,** attorney, therapist, and mediator; author of *Splitting: Protecting Yourself While Divorcing Someone with Borderline or Narcissistic Personality Disorder*

"The first book of its kind, written by an industry pioneer, *Divorcing the House* not only helps couples facing divorce, but Laurel also gives valuable insight for real estate professionals who work in these sensitive situations."

—**BEN KINNEY,** CEO, ActiveRain; Wall Street Journal
Top 100 Realtors; author of *Soci@l*;
Inman News "Innovator of the Year" 2014

"This book is a must read for anyone facing divorce and professionals who represent them. Laurel Starks has done her homework and has unprecedented experience in the field of divorce real estate. *Divorcing the House* provides great insight into family dynamics, and unlike any other book I have seen, it addresses a deeply fundamental issue: the children's concerns when leaving their home as a result of a divorce. The practical advice in these pages is invaluable."

—**ANN BINGHAM-NEWMAN,** PhD,
child psychologist, professor emeritus,
California State University–Los Angeles

DIVORCING
THE
HOUSE

A Guide to Understanding Your Options,
the Pitfalls & Whether You Could—
or Should—Keep Your Home in Divorce

LAUREL STARKS

UNHOOKED BOOKS
an imprint of High Conflict Institute Press
Scottsdale, Arizona

Copyright © 2016 by Laurel Starks
Unhooked Books, LLC
7701 E. Indian School Rd., Ste. F
Scottsdale, AZ 85251
www.unhookedbooks.com

ISBN: 978-1-936268- 97-9
eISBN: 978-1-936268-98-6

Library of Congress Control Number: 2015937571
Cover design by Gordan Blazevik
Interior layout by Jeffrey Fuller

Printed in the United States of America

Contents

Foreword

Margaret Atwood has said: "A divorce is like an amputation: you survive it, but there's less of you."

In addition to the emotional impact of losing both the dream and reality of an intact family (regardless of how dysfunctional), many divorcing couples face the reality that they no longer can live in the home they found, improved with their creativity and sweat, sacrificed to pay for, established bonds with their neighbors, live within a cherished school district, and planned to live in it until retirement or until it could be sold at the right time to fund other needs and desires.

When people separate, many fear the loss of their house/home and that fear can fuel aggressive actions that can harm everyone in the family.

Most people going through a divorce know that they need to learn more about law from lawyers, parenting from therapists, and finances from accountants and financial advisors. With this book, Laurel Starks provides focused information about how to reduce harmful conflict and maximize life choices by learning more about most family's most valuable asset: the family home.

Laurel has earned the right to author this book. A successful real estate broker with a trained caring staff aligned with a successful national franchise, Laurel is far more than a salesperson trying to earn a commission. Trained in mediation (she excelled in both my basic and advanced mediation courses) and collaborative practice, Laurel has written this book to give divorcing parties the information and insight they need to navigate decisions about their home. Some examples include:

From a market-based perspective, how do you make a decision to sell, buy out a spouse's interest, or own a house jointly?

How do handle the biggest debt in your life—your current mortgage—and how can you get financing to stay in the housing market?

What can you expect to be deducted from your proceeds in escrow, if you do decide to sell? (Laurel lists thirteen types of deductions made from the sales price.)

And much, much more . . .

Although I have been practicing law for over forty-two years, I found new insights and information on almost every page of this book. While reading this book has enhanced my ability to advise my clients regarding their home decisions, I will still recommend that they read *Divorcing the House* themselves and align themselves with a real estate professional such as Laurel Starks.

—Forrest (Woody) S. Mosten
Mediator, collaborative lawyer, and author
www.MostenMediation.com

CHAPTER ONE

When Reality Hits

There is a moment in the life of anyone getting a divorce when reality hits home: *This is really happening. I'm getting divorced.* Whether you're the one who initiated the breakup or the one on the receiving end, you'll eventually face this, and it can happen anytime during the process. For some, it's a jolt of the highest magnitude; for others it's something that's been building for a long time, and may even come as a welcome release. You may be glad your marriage is finally over, but you'll still feel the impact of that moment. It will be important then to keep your perspective: You *will* get through it—and if you make the right choices, *you will be okay.*

I got my first glimpse of this early in my career as a real estate agent. By chance, one of my very first listings was a divorce case. Some local attorneys had asked me to put a home on the market for a divorcing couple. Like many splits, this one was messy: Greg had been an abusive husband during the couple's fourteen years together, but Sarah had stayed with him—right up to the point where he moved out to be with his new girlfriend.

Greg's choices made their divorce inevitable, and by the time I entered the picture it was basically a done deal. Being a new agent, I was excited to have a listing, and so I put all my energy into marketing the house. Within a few days we received an offer. I was proud of myself and knew the attorneys would be relieved. I called Sarah to tell her the good news. Instead of relief or joy, her response was . . . silence. Then she began to weep. Soon she was sobbing uncontrollably over the phone.

I was stunned. And for the first time I realized the depth of the tragedy I was dealing with. This woman's life was disintegrating before her eyes. With my phone call, reality came crashing down on her like a tidal wave.

That was a pivotal event in my career, and my life. As an agent who now specializes in divorce sales, I've handled hundreds of such cases since then. Yet, that early experience taught me to be much more sensitive to how these events affect real people. Much of my business comes from family law professionals who call me when a couple is splitting and their home needs to be sold. By that time the divorce is usually a foregone conclusion, but as with Sarah, it can take a while for the parties to absorb its full impact. And that is true even for the person who initiates the divorce.

A Complex Process

At least three processes are occurring simultaneously during a divorce: a legal process, a real estate process, and an emotional process. All three are new to most people, and in a divorce they're all happening at the same time. It's easy to see why the experience is so wrenching. Legal matters are always daunting for the layperson; few of us go to court more than a couple of times in our lives, and virtually nobody enjoys the experience. The process of selling a home may be slightly more familiar, but it is still stressful in the best of circumstances. And ending a relationship through divorce is usually new terrain, accompanied by its own riot of emotions. Together, these ingredients can make for an overwhelmingly traumatic experience.

The situation becomes more complex when one partner is far along in the emotional process but the other is still trying to make sense of it all. By the time divorce rears its head, the initiating party may have already worked through the emotions of separation, while the other party might think everything can still work out. Joyce Tessier is a collaborative divorce coach and a marriage and family therapist in Southern California. Here's how she describes the disconnect that sometimes occurs between divorcing spouses:

> There's always a difference in pacing. There's one person that shows up and has been dealing with this for months, and they're emotionally ready. And the other guy's going, "What? You want a divorce?" Now, you're talking about two processes that are not parallel; you've got one who's ahead of the game and they're pushing for what's the next thing that's going to happen, and they're so focused on getting out of the marriage that there's not enough time for them to be in the process itself.

That process forces changes in people. And if one person is resisting it, tension can result. Tessier elaborates: "The process itself—the time—changes them . . . dealing with the facts, and the emotions . . . then you've got the other one at the starting gate, grieving because it wasn't their decision."

Often the emotional side of the process drives the other two. In their bitterness, people may seek to win at any cost. The ensuing power struggles can cloud their vision and lead to bad decisions. The house becomes a trophy that both sides strive to keep, even

5

when selling it would lead to the best outcome for everyone. In a different way, the emotional process sometimes lags behind the others. Once the machinery of divorce is set in motion, it takes on a momentum of its own. The spouses separate, hire lawyers, and then mechanically follow the directions they're given by attorneys or judges. So, the process hurtles forward, though both may secretly believe that it's all going to go away and things will return to normal. Nevertheless, eventually they find themselves standing before a family law judge, who will make decisions that affect the rest of their lives. At this point, many people are seized with anguish or panic when they realize what's happening to them.

For people who don't encounter it every day, the legal environment can seem strange, foreign, and fraught with nasty surprises. I'm fortunate to be part of a network of professionals who have unique insight into that world. This group includes attorneys, judges, mediators, therapists, loan officers, and credit experts among others. To provide a complete picture of what you could be facing, I've included insights from these professionals in this book. One of those experts is Pamela Edwards-Swift, an attorney and certified family law specialist who practices in Southern California. She is deeply familiar with the misconceptions that people often bring to the divorce process. One example: Many don't understand that when a divorce is filed, the court immediately assumes broad control over all jointly held assets. In legal parlance, these are collectively referred to as the *community*—a term that encompasses everything pertaining to the marriage. But the court's control doesn't end there. Some divorcing spouses are surprised to find that *all* their assets have been frozen—even those not related to the marriage in any way. Edwards-Swift explains:

What they don't know is that they [the courts] also have jurisdiction over *separate* property assets. For instance, when a petition is filed there are automatic temporary restraining orders that prevent a party from selling or disposing of not just community property, but also separate property. So, they're thinking, *Well, it's mine; I had it before marriage, so therefore I can do whatever I want with it.* And that's not true.

As Edwards-Swift notes, those separate assets may be needed to pay reimbursements ordered by the court. Or, the non-owner spouse may have an indirect interest:

Maybe you have somebody that owned a home before they got married and they've never changed the character of that; it's still their separate property residence. Well, because the community has made mortgage payments on that house, the community does have an interest. It may not be a large interest, but they do have some interest.

The court can also order a couple's house to be sold whether both spouses want it or not. That typically happens in the trial phase of a divorce, but it can occur beforehand under pressing circumstances—such as when the house is facing foreclosure.

Facing Reality

If you have already worked through the emotional issues of your breakup, you may be anxious to get it over with, and selling the house is the last piece of that puzzle. But for others, facing the imminent sale of the family home can be a sobering experience. It's then that they realize what they're losing, and some remain in denial right up to the last moment. The judge has ordered a sale; the house is in escrow; and they need to move out by next Friday—but they're still hanging on. They can't accept that it's over and they must begin building a new life; they're simply not ready yet. All the mundane tasks they must now undertake become fraught with emotion: finding a place to rent, having the utilities turned on in their own name, opening new bank accounts, applying for credit cards as a newly single person. It's a disorienting process under the best of circumstances. In the wake of a life-changing upheaval such as divorce, it can be crushing.

When a home is being sold, it's not just a physical structure that's at stake, or even the money it represents. A home is the brick and mortar of a family's life. It's where dreams are born— and children, too. It's where the kids grew up, and the proud parents marked their growth on the doorjambs. It's where the Christmas tree went up every year, and family gatherings took place. Most couples remember that happy day when they bought their home, whether it was a move-up purchase or a first-time venture. It was a mark of achievement that symbolized the family's future together. They had worked and saved, and that home was the fruit of their efforts. It contained their hopes, their aspirations, their life. And now, suddenly, it's all gone. In my experience, *everyone* underestimates the impact that loss will have on them.

Of course, a house can also be a reminder of painful memories: It might be where the fights occurred—or an affair. For most people the thought of home stirs up a mix of positive and negative emotions. Yet, even in the worst cases, most people aren't prepared to see it all taken away in an instant. As the process grinds on, they're often distracted by the flurry of external events, and they repress the deep changes that are occurring inside them. When their emotions finally catch up to reality, the experience can be overwhelming. I often witness this as the person designated to handle the sale of the property. Sometimes the gravity of it all hits when they make that first phone call or sit down with me in the office. It's not uncommon for people to call me and say, "I've had your number for months, but it's taken me till now to call you." I understand their reluctance; it's a big step to acknowledge that a marriage is ending and then to begin taking action. For others, the moment comes when the sale is done and we're ready to close escrow. They might have been totally cooperative throughout the process, but when it's time to sign the final paperwork, they freeze.

The Sign in the Yard

For Maggie, the reality hit her one day as she was driving her two kids home from school. She had had a beautiful home and a storybook marriage. Then suddenly, her husband decided he didn't want to be a family man after all. The kids knew that Dad had moved out and that their parents were splitting up, but they hadn't been told that their home was about to be sold. As they rounded the corner and approached the house that day, the kids spotted the for sale sign in the front yard. It was painful and jarring—not only for the children, but for Maggie as well. Suddenly she realized that she really was going to be moving.

None of it was a surprise to her, of course. She was involved in putting the house on the market and knew what was coming, but it hadn't seemed real to her until just then. She immediately got on the phone and insisted that we put the brakes on everything. She needed a little time to regroup. Her reaction was one my colleagues and I were all too familiar with. We approached Maggie's crisis with respect and compassion, and helped her get back on track.

Second Thoughts

Divorcing spouses sometimes experience second thoughts at some point in the process, even when they're the ones who initiated the split. Maybe, after eyeing the grass on the other side of the fence for years, they finally jumped over—and found out it wasn't so green. In other cases, they're not quite sure they really want to sever the cord forever; they'd like to keep their options open.

Even though my job requires me to remain neutral, I'm still affected by the human tragedies I witness. Tony and Joanne had married young and worked hard to build a business together. Over the years they gradually achieved success and were finally able to purchase some land in the foothills of Southern California. There they built their dream house and settled in to raise their four kids. It was everything a multi-million-dollar home should be, complete with crystal chandeliers and breathtaking views all the way to Catalina Island. They were the picture of a successful family. Then after the kids had grown and moved out, Joanne had a chance encounter with an old boyfriend, and a flame was rekindled. Soon she had left her husband to relive the excitement of youthful romance. Tony was devastated, but eventually came to accept that his marriage was over and he needed to move on with his life. So he struck up a new relationship of his own.

The Disappearing Spouse

Meanwhile, after a few months Joanne discovered that her fling wasn't so wonderful anymore. She wanted her old life back, but by now it was too late. Divorce was inevitable, which meant both of them would lose the dream home they had built together. Joanne proceeded to do what many wounded, confused partners do in this situation: She disappeared. For several weeks I couldn't reach her, and neither could her lawyer. Of course, that brought much of the process to a halt—but only temporarily.

By this time, Tony was the one eager to wrap up the process. He hadn't originally wanted a divorce but had acquiesced reluctantly. Now, after enduring an emotional nightmare, he was being held hostage financially by Joanne's stalling. Tony was making the mortgage payments on their former home and was paying her monthly support. On top of that he had ongoing attorney fees to take care of. Joanne was bleeding him dry, and his balance sheet was suffering more and more with every month that went by. He was counting on this sale to regain financial stability. The marriage he had once cherished—and the home that embodied it—had become a ball and chain that he desperately needed to be free of. The court was also growing impatient with the delays; the case was fast reaching a crisis stage.

Eventually Joanne appeared in my office, distraught. We managed to discuss some necessary business items, and then she began to bare her heart. The more she contemplated her tragic folly, the more she was filled with remorse. Finally she broke down. "I can't believe what I'm walking away from!" she sobbed. "I can't believe what I did to myself!"

That tendency to withdraw in the face of unbearable trauma is actually very common among the clients I work with. In almost all the cases our office handles, one or both spouses will disappear from the process at some point, if only for a little while. This is obviously a defensive reflex; people need time and space to grapple with the new reality that's been thrust upon them. Their thoughts may focus on any of several realizations:

It's really over.

She's really not coming back.

I don't have a home to go back to anymore.

I have to start over from scratch. What am I going to do now?

Without a doubt, these can all be tough changes that take a while to absorb. Yet, for the people working to help their clients get through these times, the disappearing act makes our work much more challenging. Real estate sales are complex transactions, with numerous documents to sign and issues to address. And when a divorce is at play, one or both of the parties may suddenly be unavailable at critical moments. They don't answer the phone or respond to emails. My team and I have learned to expect this and, fortunately, have developed tools and techniques over the years to deal with it. This allows us to work through the delays and achieve the results that the parties need.

When it's actually time to sell the family residence, many people are surprised by the emotional attachments they still have. There's a sense of finality about selling the home that can be hard to face. Even when one party has moved out prior to the divorce, some level of interaction usually continues. The *out-spouse* may find comfort in knowing there's a place to come back to from time to time. And the *in-spouse* may harbor hopes that the wandering partner will return someday. When the house is sold, those hopes are understandably dashed.

As one who sees the impact of this experience on real lives

every day, I offer this advice: Do not to try to deal with it alone. The consequences at every level are too immense for even the strongest, wisest person to handle. As we noted, divorce affects several aspects of your life at once. The emotional impact may seem obvious, but it can take years to fully reveal itself. Thankfully, there are competent, compassionate therapists who can help you work through your emotions. The legal and financial consequences are just as important, and you should seek wise professionals in those fields to help you plan. And the decisions concerning the house you once shared—so easy to neglect or mishandle in a time of stress—are nearly as important as anything else you will face. Handled correctly, the decisions you make now can restore the stability that will be important for your family's future.

Whether you wanted the divorce or not, the experience can be an opportunity to begin building a better life. Make the most of it by reaching out: Seek help, and seek it early.

CHAPTER TWO

Married to the Mortgage

"That's impossible."

Sam was sitting in my office reacting to the bad news I had just delivered: He wasn't going to be able to buy the house he wanted. The problem had to do with his previous home—the one he had owned with his ex-wife, Doris. It seemed like a lifetime ago.

"I gave up that house three years ago! It was part of the divorce!"

Indeed, Sam had given Doris the house by mutual agreement as part of their divorce settlement. He signed over the title and walked away, and he thought he was done with it. But now the home was in foreclosure, and it was showing up on his credit report. Just when he was ready to launch into a new life, Sam's old life was pulling him back and wouldn't let go. He was not happy.

Sam had made a mistake common among many divorcing spouses: He had ended his marriage and given his ex-spouse their home—but he was still married to the mortgage. If you're puzzled about how that could happen, you're not alone. It all has to do with the difference between ownership and debt obligations.

When you purchase a home, you usually assume ownership through a *grant deed*. This document identifies you as the new owner, and it is normally recorded in the official records of the county where the property is located. The deed may identify you as a *sole and separate* owner or, if you're married, it may show both you and your spouse as co-owners. Many homeowners have not even glanced at this piece of paper, but it is the only document that proves they own their home.

At the time of the purchase you made a choice regarding whose name would be on that title document and what form of ownership to adopt. There are several ways for spouses to hold title together. Common forms of shared ownership include *joint tenancy, community property,* and *community property with right of survivorship*. Real estate may also be owned by a partnership, trust, or corporation.

When one party surrenders ownership rights to another, this is normally done through a *quitclaim deed*. When the transfer is between spouses, as in a divorce settlement, an *interspousal transfer deed* is often the preferred instrument.

Title versus Mortgage

The loan you took out to purchase the property is a completely separate instrument from the title, and may include a different set of names. The document that obligates a borrower to repay the loan is called the *note*. One or both spouses may be signers on the note. If one has better credit and sufficient income to qualify for the loan, that party may be the only signer. If both spouses' incomes are necessary to qualify, both will sign. (The *mortgage,* or *trust deed,* is a separate document that provides the house as collateral in the event of default. But the loan itself is commonly referred to as the *mortgage,* so we'll continue that practice in these discussions.)

Here's the most important point: Signing over the title to the house does not affect who is on the mortgage. If you were a signer on the loan, you're still responsible for that obligation until it's paid off.

Even when the court orders one spouse to surrender ownership to the other, the loan remains in force. As powerful as the family court is, it doesn't have authority to alter your loan, which is a private contract. You can march down to the bank with your court order and say, "The judge ordered my spouse to take care of all this!" but it won't change anything. If your name is on the loan, you remain responsible.

Does that come as news to you? If so, you're in good company. Most people are unaware of this distinction. Attorney Pamela Edwards-Swift deals regularly with clients who are misinformed on this topic. As she observes, "One of the biggest things up that comes up, surprisingly, is that they think all they have to do is sign an interspousal transfer deed signing the property over to the other spouse, and automatically that takes them off of the loan. That's a really big problem. And that comes up a lot."

It's distressing enough that most divorcing spouses don't understand this, but here's a secret: Many attorneys overlook this as well. That's why people such as Sam, who signed over his house and thought he was done with it, are surprised when the old mortgage comes back to bite them. Even *judges* sometimes miss the fact that removing someone from the title doesn't remove them from the loan. I know this because I regularly take their calls and answer their questions. It's why I also spend a lot of time educating legal professionals on real estate matters through seminars, articles, and other media. In their defense, attorneys and judges typically handle multiple cases at once and are juggling a huge range of issues in each one: child custody, child support, financial arrangements, and domestic violence concerns—just to name a few. Sometimes, the details of the real estate transactions are simply not on their radar.

Yet misconceptions on this issue can cause a variety of problems for either spouse: As in Sam's case, being a signer on an existing mortgage may prevent you from obtaining a new one. You'll have a hard time moving forward as long as that obligation exists. People in this situation understandably grow tired of being stuck and seek relief in the courts. At that point the in-spouse may be at risk: The court can order the house to be sold—whether the in-spouse wants it or not.

As both parties may be dismayed to discover, they're still married—to the mortgage, that is. This can remain so even years after the divorce is final.

It's very common for the out-spouse to quitclaim the house to the in-spouse without addressing the mortgage issue. That person is then in the unenviable position of being financially liable for a home he or she doesn't own. The in-spouse may not have the financial means to maintain the mortgage. This can sometimes be remedied through a spousal support (alimony) arrangement, but even then the in-spouse may simply choose not to make the payments, out of spite or sheer incompetence. In a worst-case scenario, the in-spouse eventually defaults on the loan, resulting in a foreclosure. Then, both parties have not only lost the house; they now have a foreclosure on their respective credit reports, which will hinder their financial activities for years. A foreclosure can yield even greater ramifications. Lenders often don't recoup the entire unpaid loan balance when they foreclose on a home. The amount that remains unpaid is called the *deficiency*. Depending on the foreclosure laws of your state, both parties may be responsible for that unpaid balance. This can especially apply to second mortgages and home equity lines of credit (HELOCs). The lender can seek a deficiency judgment from a court and then pursue the parties through a variety of means: confiscating assets, garnishing wages, or even seizing proceeds from future home sales.

In some divorce cases, one spouse moves out but the financial and legal relationships regarding the house are left unchanged; both parties remain on title as well as on the loan. A spouse may be willing to leave, but unwilling to relinquish ownership of a house he or she is still financially responsible for. This arrangement can create its own problems. In a familiar scenario, the husband leaves the home but remains on title, while the ex-wife stays in the home to raise the children. While Mom may feel secure in this arrangement, Dad may be incurring additional debts in his life that end up as liens on the property. When a debt is unpaid, the creditor may file a *personal lien* against the debtor. This lien then attaches to anything the debtor owns— including real estate. The unsuspecting ex-spouse can be in for a rude surprise when it's time to sell the house or refinance. That lien must be dealt with one way or another.

As these examples illustrate, it's not enough to divorce the unwanted spouse; you should also divorce the house!

Getting Free

Put simply, the only way to remove your name from a loan is to pay it off. This can be accomplished in one of two ways: by refinancing or by selling.

A refinance involves obtaining an entirely new loan to replace the old one. The original loan is paid off, and the new one may have different terms and different signers. Although this can be an effective way to remove one party from the mortgage, there are obstacles: It will be difficult to qualify for refinancing if the remaining spouse can't demonstrate an ability to repay the new loan. And if the house does not have the level of equity most lenders require for a cushion, refinancing may not be an option.

In recent years *loan modifications* have become very common. This tool allows distressed homeowners to keep their homes through lowered payments; sometimes the actual principal balance is reduced. Usually, the homeowner must demonstrate a verifiable hardship—which is not difficult for most divorcing spouses. However, the process is long and requires extensive documentation and approval by the lender's underwriting team. Many modification requests are denied the first time. Nevertheless, when a modification is approved with realistic terms, it can allow people to keep their homes.

What a loan modification *won't* do in most cases is remove a signer's name from the loan. In a modification, the existing loan remains intact. The terms are changed—but usually not the borrowers. Spouses who look to a modification as a way to untangle their shared finances are bound for disappointment.

In many cases, a sale is the only practical option. That can be painful to consider, but if it's the inevitable outcome, it's best to face it early on. A skilled attorney will gently present the facts and let the clients make their own informed choices. Here's how attorney Pamela Edwards-Swift handles such situations: "It is something that I will talk to my clients about," and if they see the logic in it, the next step is "seeing if we can get the other side to agree to list it for sale sooner rather than later, if that's the avenue that they know they have to go down, and before they get themselves into trouble financially." As she points out, it's important to act quickly when the way forward is clear. Delaying the process can drain both parties' finances as they try to sustain unmanageable payments. The home can fall into foreclosure, making a bad situation much worse.

For almost everyone, the financial impact of divorce is a sobering reality that cannot be avoided. The ex-spouses must now sustain two households on income that used to support one. That often means a drastic reduction in lifestyle. If it is clearly impossible for one spouse to maintain the house payments, the parties can agree to sell, or the court may order a sale. In either case, the loan is disposed.

That becomes more complicated when the sale proceeds are less than the amount owed. In such cases the parties must seek the lender's approval for a *short sale*. (We'll talk in-depth about short sale transactions in chapter 7.)

If the scenarios we've described so far seem challenging, they can become even more complex when there is more than one loan on a property. Many homes today are encumbered by a first mortgage, a second mortgage, and maybe an additional home equity line of credit. A spouse may be a signer on one loan, but not the others. I routinely counsel clients who tell me, "Oh yeah, I'm on the loan!" And with a little research we learn that they're not. Most such homeowners don't have a clear recollection of who signed what; many don't even know how many loans their property has.

Needless to say, resolving these situations requires investigation. The first thing I do when I meet with a potential client—even if it's just a consultation—is order a *preliminary title report* from a reputable title company. I want to know who the players are and what positions they're playing. This report will show clearly the encumbrances on the property. Then we can begin to formulate a realistic strategy to resolve each one.

Real estate transactions are complex by nature, and even more so when they're part of a divorce. That's why I've developed useful relationships with numerous family law professionals. They recognize that the real estate aspect of a divorce is terribly important but that it's beyond the scope of their responsibility and skill set. A specialist in divorce real estate matters can identify potential pitfalls and help you avoid them. That can be a great source of comfort when you're in the midst of a distressing and vulnerable period of life.

CHAPTER THREE

To Sell, or Not to Sell?

Should you sell your family home? The place where you and your partner invested your lives; where your children grew up and experienced their important milestones; where you laughed, loved, struggled, and quarreled over the years?

This is one of the most wrenching—and important—decisions that a divorcing couple must make. Since that home is probably the most valuable asset you own, the financial consequences are huge—but, of course, so are the emotional implications. That's why it's so important to carefully think through all of the issues involved. The expert advice of competent professionals will be indispensable in this process. Attorneys, financial counselors, therapists, Realtors—all can provide essential counsel that will help your planning. Engaging a number of advisors at this point may seem expensive, but considering the stakes, it could turn out to be a bargain. You are also gaining critical insights from reading this book. It incorporates the views of experts from several disciplines and may expose you to valuable information you wouldn't have considered otherwise. Do yourself a favor and hold off on making any permanent decisions until you finish it! This chapter will outline the various factors that can influence your decisions, and later chapters will examine each of those issues in depth.

The decision you're facing may be difficult, but it's not complicated. In the final analysis, you really only have three options:

1. Keep the house and leave the title and mortgage as they are.
2. Transfer the title and mortgage to one partner.
3. Sell the house.

Each of these choices may be attractive for different reasons, but they may not all be feasible. The first question you must ask is: Can either party afford to keep the house under any scenario? Answering that will require a hard look at the numbers. If the answer is no, your decision is clear: You must sell.

Remember, you're now going to be supporting two households with the same income that previously supported one. Will that really be enough to sustain the current home plus another one? Many families are stretched to the limit trying to make their existing house payments. Adding another payment—even a modest one—is out of the question. If that is your situation, you'll be better off coming to grips with reality early on. Then you can begin strategizing to make your transition as orderly and pain-free as possible.

Of course, things are not always black-and-white. You may be uncertain about the future, but optimistic. Getting through your ordeal to this point has probably required a lot of positive thinking, and you may feel inspired to take on another challenge. You tell yourself, *I think I can make it work!* That's a good attitude, but it must be balanced by reality. This chapter will explore things to consider as you envision your future.

Where's My Support?

If you plan on staying in the house, will you be counting on either spousal support or child support to make it work? If so, how reliable is your ex-spouse? You may have a court order mandating payments of a certain amount; that doesn't guarantee you will actually receive the money. It's not uncommon for exes to withhold payments out of spite. On the other hand, many ex-partners have every intention of making their payments but find that they simply can't. Circumstances may have changed, or the arrangement may have been unrealistic to begin with.

Your ex could be laid off or fired without warning. Is he or she an artist? A construction contractor? Self-employed people are vulnerable to wide swings in income. Moreover, the most common form of support is child support—which may end once the children become legal adults. If Johnny is seventeen and Suzie is sixteen, your income could be decreasing soon. Better to avoid making long-term plans based on that payment arrangement. The bottom line: If your future depends on a shaky income source, it's wise to plan conservatively.

A Slave to the House

You might be hoping to keep the house, for any number of good reasons. But things have changed now. The home that was once a source of security could become a nuisance very quickly. You won't just be making the loan payment; you'll be covering property taxes and insurance too. (For many homeowners, taxes and insurance are included in their monthly payments to the mortgage company, but you'll need to verify that for your case.) Your home's value might be increasing, which is a good thing. But that probably means your property tax is increasing too.

You'll also need to set aside money for maintenance. Is the house showing its age? That implies another set of issues: What shape is the plumbing in? The wiring? How about the roof? These are concerns you may not have needed to think about when you had a partner. Now, you'll have to. Who's going to care for the yard? Is there a pool? Have you figured the pool maintenance expense into your budget? You'll also be paying for utilities on a house that may be bigger than you need. Take all these issues into consideration as you formulate your plans—and put a dollar figure on each one.

Even if you are financially able to handle all these contingencies, you must ask yourself one question: Is it worth it? You might take on the challenge, only to find that you've become a slave, working endlessly for the privilege of saying that you *kept the house*. Meanwhile, you're incurring an opportunity cost, since the money you're pouring into the house isn't available for other things. Will you have money to put away for the kids' college? Will you have to forgo vacations for the foreseeable future? How many field trips will your kids have to skip because you couldn't afford the cost? Will they be able to get those braces they need? What about sports uniforms, cheerleader's outfits, and the thousand other needs that inevitably crop up?

As you contemplate these things, you may conclude that a smaller, newer house can meet your needs more efficiently without the headaches. Most people buy homes that match their needs at the time. If your family unit is now reduced by one or more members, it may be a good time to downsize.

Condominiums remain a popular form of homeownership, because they provide amenities that people desire without the associated stress. There is usually a homeowners' association that handles external maintenance issues, and the expense is shared among the association members. That can be a welcome relief in a time of transition. Of course, the convenience is accompanied by a monthly dues payment. But this is money you might have spent anyway with a traditional single family home—for yard care, repairs, and other maintenance expenses.

What Do You Really Want?

For some people, the home is an important emotional anchor, and holding on to it becomes an all-consuming need. But for others, the house represents mostly bad memories, and letting go of it is the most therapeutic thing they can do. Sandra was one of my clients who decided to sell her house after discovering her husband had used it as a trysting place for his numerous mistresses. Since that betrayal, she couldn't bear even to drive down the street where they had once lived. In truth, she had come to hate that house. Selling it was cause for celebration! You must ask yourself, *What do I really want?* After the divorce, will you be able to come back to that same house every day and still move forward with your life? If it will be more of an emotional burden than a blessing, your choice is made for you.

Reaching a decision on this all-important issue will require some honest introspection, away from the pressures of everyday life. You may also need to separate yourself from the advice that flows so freely from others when couples are splitting up. What you discover then may surprise you. Perhaps keeping the house isn't that important after all. Getting a fresh start may be a higher priority.

Often, the in-spouse will opt to hold on to the house "for the kids" until they're grown. According to this line of thought, they've been through enough upheaval already; remaining in a familiar environment will provide at least some semblance of stability. This is a noble sentiment that reflects the best intentions of a responsible parent. But it may not be the perfect solution. Knee-jerk reactions don't always yield the best results. Don't presume that you know what your kids want or what will ultimately be best for them. Determining that will require some in-depth probing, perhaps with some expert help.

Buying Out the Other Spouse

As we described earlier, the worst possible scenario is for one partner to transfer the title to the other while remaining responsible for the loan (or loans). This can lead to prolonged heartache and stress, if not disaster. That's why we don't include it as a viable option. But there are cases in which it is possible to sever the legal and financial ties while still allowing one spouse to keep the house. This is typically done through refinancing.

In this arrangement, an entirely new loan is issued to replace the old one. The catch is that the in-spouse must be able to qualify for the loan. As an example: Bob and Jessica agree that she will keep their house, which is worth $400,000. It is encumbered by loans of $300,000, so the net equity is $100,000. In a typical divorce, the jointly held assets are split evenly, so Bob would be entitled to $50,000 of that equity. (One of the benefits of this arrangement is that the money goes directly to Bob through the settlement process; there is no possibility that the funds will be diverted or "forgotten".) Jessica, then, needs to secure a new loan for $350,000 to pay off the old loan and give Bob his share of the equity. Will she be able to afford the payments on that increased amount? That is the question she must answer, and which the lender will be examining closely. Denise Fontyn is a loan underwriter and manager for Provident Bank. She often works with divorcing spouses who are grappling with this issue. "Sometimes," she says, "one of them really wants to stay in the property and buy the other one out. And that's what they're adamant about." They may qualify for the loan but then have second thoughts when they see the numbers. Fontyn continues, "Once I show them on paper, 'Look, if you buy them out, this is what your payment's going to be'—they don't want to pay that much. It's above their budget."

In some cases, the spouses may agree to trade the equity in the house for some other jointly held assets: Bob might agree to surrender his equity in the house in exchange for the couple's $100,000 stock portfolio. But Jessica would still need to refinance $300,000 to remove Bob from the loan—and then be able to make the monthly payments. Arrangements of this type are common among couples who hold substantial assets together. In such an agreement, fixed dollar amounts must be assigned to all the assets they own together. Then, the parties can agree to an equitable division, or if the case goes to court, the judge will order one at his or her discretion. In *community property* states such as California, the value of all jointly held assets must be divided absolutely evenly. This is achieved through a process of *equalization*, in which the value of all assets is calculated and divided 50-50. Other states may allow more flexibility, so long as the arrangement is deemed equitable.

But most divorcing spouses have only a few large assets to divide, with the house being the primary one. So, the proper settlement of the house is crucial to both parties. Oddly, when divorce cases go to trial, the house is often treated as a secondary issue. Courts typically focus on child custody and support issues first, and the house can be put on the back burner—the one asset that should provide the financial bedrock for both ex-partners. This makes it all the more important for *you*, as one of the divorcing parties, to take up the slack and treat the house with the care it deserves.

What happens when there is no equity to divide? As we'll discuss more fully in chapter 7, this is a reality for many homeowners in today's real estate market. Often, divorcing partners reflexively defend their rights to the house, when an objective analysis would reveal that there's nothing to fight over: The house is underwater. Denise Fontyn sees this dynamic often with clients as they haggle over a house that has no equity. "They don't realize it's not an asset," she observes. "It's a complete liability to them." In such cases the sensible course would be to liquidate the obligation as painlessly as possible. That usually means pursuing a short sale, which we'll discuss in detail later.

For some divorcing homeowners, buying out the other spouse is the obvious right choice. This is feasible when there is substantial equity in the house, and the person can qualify for a loan. Barbara was a prospective client who called me about listing her house for sale. We met at the property and she took me on a tour. It was a well-appointed, comfortable home and I knew it would sell at a good price. In our conversation, she revealed that she owed only $70,000 on the mortgage. As we walked together I began to mull over her situation.

Finally, I asked her, "What's your goal?"

"Well," she sighed, "I'd really like to keep the house."

"Then, let's work to make that happen."

Barbara was ideally positioned to keep her home: She could refinance, pulling out enough money to pay her husband his share, and still have a reasonable house payment—far lower than what she would pay to rent another home. Her children wouldn't need to adjust to a new home, and she could stay in the house she loved.

Getting a New Loan

Unfortunately, not all divorcing spouses are as well positioned as Barbara. We've described the burden of obtaining a loan large enough to pay off a spouse's equity interest. Ironically, the more equity there is, the larger the burden on the partner seeking a new loan. But apart from that, several surprises may await the newly single person. You may find that not only is your financial strength reduced with the divorce, but the lending environment has changed since you last went through the loan process.

The easy-money lending policies of the early twenty-first century led to an unprecedented financial crisis, with effects that persisted into the following decade. In response, lenders tightened their guidelines drastically. Many longtime homeowners are surprised to learn that they can't obtain financing in the new environment. Those who can are confronted with a bewildering array of products, with different provisions, interest rates, and charges. Moreover, the rates and guidelines are constantly shifting. This is why it's essential to find a capable loan officer who is forthright and communicative, and who understands the market.

It's also important to find out what you qualify for *before* any decisions about your existing home are set in stone. In her role as an underwriter, Denise Fontyn reviews loan applications from countless would-be borrowers and their eager loan officers. She is continually dismayed with how many people make plans without bothering to find out whether they can actually qualify for a loan. "I'm really shocked that more people don't get a consultation to find out what they can and can't do—before they even go to court," she says. As we've noted, the court doesn't have authority over everything. A judge may order the remaining spouse to refinance the loan, but even a judge can't make the impossible possible. "Regardless of what a court order says, it's irrelevant to a loan person," Denise observes. "If you don't qualify, you don't qualify. And if your credit's not there, you're not getting a loan." As the saying goes, look before you leap.

If You Stay

We've outlined the various challenges in keeping the house after a divorce and factors to consider when making this decision.

Nevertheless, keeping the house is still the right option for many. If that is the direction you are leaning, taking a few precautionary steps will help ensure your peace of mind:

Get a home inspection. A professional home inspector will examine all the systems in the house and help you track down problems before they become obvious emergencies. That will give you a more realistic idea of what you'll be facing if you keep the house. Plumbing, wiring, insulation, the roof, the foundation, the structure itself—any of these may present problems that can suck you dry financially. It's wise to know what you're dealing with sooner rather than later, before your decision regarding the house is final. The last thing you need at this point is to inherit a stack of potentially expensive troubles.

Get a home warranty. These are the policies that sellers routinely provide for homebuyers to enhance their comfort level in a purchase. Real estate agents regularly work with home warranty companies, so if you have a relationship with a good Realtor, ask for a referral. Home warranties typically cover most repair issues—with a reasonable service fee per visit. But they may also exclude some types of repairs—such as air conditioning or roofing—so examine your policy carefully.

Get a life insurance policy. It's a grim thought, but if you're relying on your ex-partner for income, you need some assurance of support if that person dies. Buy an insurance policy on your ex-spouse and on yourself if you have children at home.

The Big Picture

The pressing decision you face regarding your house also presents a unique opportunity to assess your entire financial picture. If you haven't yet done so, this would be a good time to consult a financial planner. If you must handle the task yourself, at least seize the moment to take a broad inventory of your situation. Amid the emotional disruption, you'll benefit by doing something completely counterintuitive: Consider your marital community as a business. This will be easy for those who are analytical and business-minded by nature—and feel completely odd to those who aren't. But approaching things this way will help you make informed, wise decisions, preparing you for the future as you rebuild your life on your own.

Start with what businesspeople would recognize as a *balance sheet*: a two-column list with your assets on one side, your liabilities on the other. For example, your house would qualify as an asset, the mortgage as a liability. Include anything with real market value on the asset side, and every obligation or debt on the liability side. The difference between the two sums is your *net worth*.

Then, compile a list of your monthly income and expenses. Include everything: house payments, utilities, food, car payments, gasoline, entertainment, and an extra amount for the unanticipated costs that seem to crop up every month. If you own a business, produce a realistic figure for what the business brings in every month, after expenses, income taxes, and self-employment taxes.

This will form the basis of your household budget—an essential part of navigating the divorce process. You now have an idea of your current financial state and can begin planning for your future. You may, like many people at this point, conclude that you need more income. Where will that money come from? And how does the house fit into that picture?

Whatever path you ultimately choose, it's wise to go in with as much information as possible. Get lots of advice. Then weigh it against what you really want. Look hard at the numbers, and don't be afraid of what you see there.

You're at the beginning of a journey. Don't rush it.

CHAPTER FOUR

What's Your House Worth, Anyway?

D o you know what your house is *really* worth—today? Many people have a vague idea, perhaps based on some nearby sales from last year or what they *heard* a neighbor's house sold for. But when a marriage is ending and it's time to start dividing assets, you need a precise, realistic figure.

If the house is your most valuable financial asset, it makes sense to handle it with the greatest care. That's especially true when making decisions at the end of a relationship. Choices made now can have profound, long-lasting effects on both parties. The brutal truth is that most divorcing spouses suffer financial hardship during the years following their breakup. Often, the only hedge against that hardship is the equity in their house. Thus, getting an accurate valuation of the house is crucial to both parties' financial well-being.

There are some obvious questions that will need to be answered early: Both parties are going to need homes to live in. Will one of them take the house? That often depends on its value and how affordable it is for the remaining spouse. If the home is sold, how much does each party expect to pocket? That depends on how much equity remains after all the sale expenses. What if there's no equity at all? In all these scenarios, obtaining an accurate valuation is vitally important—and the sooner, the better.

Janet found that out the hard way. She and her husband owned their home and a business together. When they divorced, they agreed that he would take the business and she would get the house. That arrangement seemed equitable—and then she decided to sell the property. When our real estate team ran the comparable sales on Janet's house, we found that it was worth about $200,000 less than she had assumed. By that time, the divorce was final and she was on her own to piece together her financial life based on whatever was left. For a while it appeared that she might end up with nothing; the property was encumbered with several loans that would all need to be settled before she could receive a penny. Fortunately we were able to negotiate settlements on all of them, and Janet came out with enough cash to move forward with her life. But it was far less than she had imagined. Meanwhile, her ex-husband was doing fine with a thriving business, which he now owned outright.

How could she have avoided such an unfair outcome? By insisting on getting a formal home valuation *before agreeing to anything.* When you're making decisions that will shape the rest of your life, vague notions and wishful thinking aren't helpful.

There are several ways to get an estimate of value on your property. Perhaps the easiest is to access one of the online services that provide free instant valuations. These can give you a quick snapshot of what other homes have sold for nearby as well as a rough value estimate of your property based on that information. They collect publicly available data and present it in an accessible, convenient form. But as these websites freely admit, their estimates are often not very reliable. An accurate valuation must incorporate a number of different factors that may not be obvious in the data. Conversely, some data may be irrelevant or extraneous, and including it will only produce distorted numbers. These online services, being automated, can't provide the personal judgment necessary to arrive at a precise figure. There is simply no substitute for having a pair of human eyes examining the data, and a discerning mind analyzing it.

A Valuation Overview

Your house is worth whatever a willing and able buyer would pay for it today. The best way to determine that is to find out what other comparable properties (comps) have sold for recently. The key words here are *comparable* and *recently*. Good comps are homes that have sold nearby with similar characteristics to yours, taking into account age, square footage, lot size, and number of bedrooms and baths. It's also important to factor in amenities such as swimming pools, spas, or upgrades—so long as they can be assigned realistic dollar values.

The most important factor in determining value is time. The value of a comp depends on how *recent* the sale was. In volatile markets prices can change almost daily; a sale may be irrelevant if it was from last month, let alone last year. Ideally, you will want to consider sales within the last three months, six months at the most. The most current sales are going to bear the most weight. What's more, since the real estate market fluctuates so rapidly and a valuation is only good for the day it was done, you will want to have the home's value reassessed closer to settlement so that it is as accurate as possible. Real estate professionals will use the most recent comps available to formulate a value.

The neighborhood is also critical. You may have heard the cliché that the three most important things in real estate are *location, location* and *location.* There's an element of truth in that. The house one block away might be part of another development that has a totally different character and reputation. If your house is in a cul-de-sac while the comp is on a busy thoroughfare, that affects its relative value. Are there apartments next door? A factory? Power transmission lines? All these affect a property's desirability. A skilled real estate professional will take them into consideration.

Size is one of the most crucial factors to consider. Among the first numbers that real estate pros look at is the square footage. This calculation only considers living space—not garages, tool sheds, or covered patios. If your next-door neighbor's house sold for $400,000, don't presume that yours will too. Check out the square footage; if his house was 4,000 square feet while yours is only 2,000, then yours will probably be worth considerably less.

The perfect way to incorporate all these factors neatly is to find a house that is a model match to yours. Even then, differences must be considered that will affect the relative value of each: improvements or lack thereof, maintenance, location, etc.

Unfortunately, the amenities in your property may not be as helpful as you think. Some improvements enhance the *desirability* of a home, but not the price. They may have great value to you, especially if you put time, sweat, and money into them, but that doesn't always translate into increased market value. Moreover, the improvements you've made may not appeal to all potential buyers. You may have just installed new granite countertops, but that won't mean much when granite falls out of fashion. Your pool may have cost you $40,000, but not all buyers want a pool. For some—especially those with small children—the pool may be considered a liability and so may not improve your sale price at all. The most important factors in determining value are the hard numbers, which are not easy to change: year built, square footage, number of bedrooms and baths, lot size.

A popular misconception is that value can be determined based on the asking prices of nearby homes. But remember, sellers can ask any price they want. What matters are *closed sales*, since they indicate what buyers have actually paid. Many times the final sale price will differ dramatically from the initial asking price.

A skilled professional will recognize trends in the prices of active listings (those still for sale) and, more particularly, in *pending* sales (those that have entered the contract phase but have not yet closed). In a fast-moving market your asking price may be adjusted according to these trends—but only with great caution. A diligent agent will call the listing agents on those pending sales to uncover the actual sale prices. That will provide a clear idea of where the market is heading, and how fast it is moving.

Buyers who aren't paying cash must rely on mortgage loans to make their purchases. And real estate lenders are normally very careful not to overpay for properties. That means your price must satisfy not just the buyer—but the buyer's lender.

With all these factors to consider, how does a homeowner obtain a reliable valuation? We've already discussed the cheapest way—the free online estimate, which is often worth exactly what you pay for it. There are two more reliable ways: the formal appraisal and the *comparative market analysis* (CMA).

The Appraisal

This report is prepared by a licensed appraiser, a professional who must spend many hours in training and apprenticeship to qualify for that designation. A lender will typically hire an appraiser when it is considering writing a loan on a particular property. In these cases, the appraisal's only function is to protect the mortgage investor—not the buyer, even though the buyer may be paying for it. If the appraisal falls significantly below the agreed sale price, the lender will require the buyer to cough up the difference in order to get the loan. Many sales are stopped cold when the appraisal comes in too low. Even if the buyer was ready and eager to pay top price for the property, lenders are typically more objective and conservative; they will rarely lend more than the appraisal warrants. Appraisers are also used when the court is disposing of a property—as in a divorce settlement. So, the appraiser's accuracy and reliability are of paramount importance.

Usually an appraiser will show up onsite with a measuring tape to ensure the accuracy of all the property dimensions listed in county records. The appraiser then uses all available property data to arrive at a conclusion, which is presented in an exhaustive report. Needless to say, appraisals cost money—normally a few hundred dollars on residential property, much more if the property is commercial or agricultural.

The CMA

A comparative market analysis is a report prepared for the homeowner by a real estate agent—typically before listing the home. The CMA is based on data regarding recent sales culled from the multiple listing service and county title records.

Agents often prepare CMAs and present them to homeowners free of charge—in hopes of earning business. The figures in the CMA are then used to set an asking price when the property is put on the market. Since the agent's success depends on an accurate valuation, these reports are typically quite reliable. They incorporate much of the same data an appraiser would use; in fact, appraisers often obtain their most current market information from agents, who may have inside knowledge on active and pending sales.

The most obvious advantage of a CMA is that it is normally free—yet offers a reliable estimate of value. Agents also have a finger on the pulse of the market in a way that even trained appraisers may not; after all, they're working with buyers and sellers every day.

As we've noted, the real value of a property is what a willing and able buyer will pay for it. Few buyers show up at a house with a tape measure and calculator, and they don't normally enter the values of the home's features in an accounting ledger. Their responses are based on more subjective things: the way the den feels, the size of the closets, the view from the backdoor sliders. If it's a two-story house, is one of the bedrooms downstairs? For some buyers, that will immediately make it more appealing—especially if it's the master bedroom. An appraiser may not consider such intangibles, but an experienced agent will.

Buyers acquainted with the Asian concept of Feng Shui may pay close attention to the home's *chi*, which can be roughly translated as energy or flow. They'll note the position of the house in relation to the surrounding geography, the landscaping, the ease of movement between the rooms. Needless to say, appraisals can't quantify these things in a report.

Subjective factors can also include negative things such as poor decorating or lapsed maintenance. Pets have been known to leave urine stains on floors and carpets—with all the accompanying aromas. Over time the homeowners may become accustomed to this, but most prospective buyers will be immediately repulsed. Again, these things won't show up in an appraisal but will nonetheless affect a home's marketability. Such a home might stay on the market longer than desired and force the homeowner to drop the price. A savvy agent will recognize these factors and consider them in proposing an asking price.

As valuable as a CMA is, it's only as good as the agent preparing it. These reports are often produced using computer programs, just as the free online reports are. A careless or inexperienced agent may simply input the data without making the necessary judgments and corrections to achieve an accurate value. Calculating a precise figure requires an agent with experience and knowledge of the area to correctly analyze the data, determining which sales are pertinent and making adjustments for variables. Make sure the agent you choose is well qualified and seasoned.

Beware also of the unscrupulous agent who presents an inflated value just to get your listing. You may be approached by someone promising, "*I can get you* such-and-such an amount." But ultimately, the market determines what a property sells for. No agent can "get you" more than the market will bear. Signing a listing agreement with a particular agent based on unrealistic expectations only wastes time, as the price will eventually have to be adjusted anyway. If the promised price is far higher than all other reasonable estimates, think twice about hiring that agent.

Since a CMA is typically free, it is wise to get one as early in the process as possible. Having a realistic idea of what your most important asset is really worth will help you in the rest of your decision-making at this time. However, remember that values change. It's not unusual for divorces to take years. And if you obtained a property valuation early in the process, you'll probably need to update it before it's all over.

The BPO

There is another type of report that mortgage servicers (banks) use when they are considering disposing of property. This is the *broker price opinion* (BPO), which is typically prepared by a real estate agent at the request of the bank. It is less thorough than a formal appraisal, and therefore less expensive. This innovative approach is a product of the recent mortgage crisis. As the volume of short sales and *real estate owned* (REO) began to increase dramatically, banks found themselves handling huge numbers of transactions at once. Since these transactions were already incurring losses for the banks, saving money became a high priority. The BPO, prepared by an agent rather than a licensed appraiser, emerged as an economical substitute for the formal appraisal.

As a homeowner, you would only encounter the BPO process in certain circumstances: Your mortgage servicer might order a BPO if you chose to pursue a short sale—a transaction in which the sale proceeds are less than the amount owed. In those cases the mortgage investor on the existing loan is taking a loss on the sale, so its approval is required to complete the transaction. It will order a BPO to determine if the proposed sale is at fair market value. When you are the homeowner, your only task in this process is to make the house available. It is to your benefit to cooperate, since your successful sale depends on the bank's approval. And when there is no equity to divide between the former spouses, you literally have nothing to lose. At any rate, some BPOs are based only on exterior, drive-by inspections, which require no effort at all on your part.

Upside-Down

Depending on the current housing market, some homeowners might not have any equity—they owe more on their homes than they could possibly get in a sale. If that may be your situation, it's better to find out now. It may be a rude awakening, but it's better than making plans based on money that will never materialize.

If you're contemplating a sale, you may already have a real estate agent in mind. That agent should be very willing to provide you with an estimate of your home's value, so you can begin making wise decisions. If the agent is skilled, it will be a solid, reliable valuation.

The bottom line: Find out your bottom line—as early as you can.

CHAPTER FIVE

The Emotion Factor

What could be more traumatic than a divorce? The feelings that accompany a breakup are chaotic and uncontrollable, often swinging wildly from one extreme to another. Therapist and divorce coach Joyce Tessier describes the experience vividly in her essay "The Emotional Divorce":

> Divorce is the second most stressful event one can experience, second only to the death of an immediate family member. The grief which follows is the natural process of emotional and life adjustment you go through after such a loss. Divorce is also the loss of the fantasy of what marriage and marital life might have been regardless of whether the separation is amicable or vindictive.
>
> A wide range of feelings are common to grieving and fill the mind with chaos and contradictory emotions. They may feel shock, numbness, sadness, anger, guilt and/ or fear. They may also find moments of relief, excitement and anticipation of new possibilities.
>
> However, the process of grief and grieving can take a physical toll on the body. Our body does not know the difference between stress that is caused by physical

factors and stress caused by emotional factors. Stress is stress.

In the midst of this disruption, divorcing parties must make a series of major decisions that will impact the rest of their lives. Needless to say, that combination creates a hazardous situation. And some of the greatest potential hazards lie in the family residence.

Here are some of the foolish things divorcing people do in this regard:

- Sign over ownership without considering the consequences (such as the remaining mortgage)
- Hold on to the house for emotional security, when it makes more sense to sell
- Fight over the house as a trophy, when there's no equity
- Spend time and money fighting over trivial items
- Insist on setting an unreasonable asking price, just to make a point
- Let the house go for too little, to be done with it
- Stop making the house payments
- Stop maintaining the house
- Refuse to sign or even look at important documents
- Refuse to leave after the house has transferred ownership

As irrational and destructive as these behaviors are, they're also understandable. Deciding whether to keep or sell the house, who gets to stay there for the time being, what price to sell at, and who gets to keep what—these would be difficult choices in any circumstances. But in the context of a breakup, they take on emotional weight that invites bad judgment calls. Most people in crisis are thinking about their short-term problems and how to get through them—not the recovery that will follow. But the decisions you make at these moments have long-term consequences. In the cases I've observed, when people act based on emotions it can delay their financial recovery by as much as seven years. By contrast, those who keep their eyes wide open, educate themselves, and seek help when they need it can recover very quickly. Your heart may be broken, but you'll still need to deal with some big issues—using your brain.

Why Did I Do That?

Emotions can lead us to do strange things, particularly when circumstances seem especially dire. It may feel as if your actions are beyond your control at these times, and in some ways they are. Most people have heard of the *fight, flight, or freeze* response. This reaction is biologically triggered in both animals and humans when faced with, or even when they sense what they think is, an emergency. This means that when confronted with danger, we're primed to run away, stand and do battle, or simply become inert and play possum. Any of these can be appropriate responses to a particular situation. But we usually revert to them at moments when they're of no use, and in doing so we actually make things worse.

Again, this mechanism is automatic in times of crisis; it is designed to get us out of danger as quickly and effectively as possible. Yet our actions, or non-actions, at this time override our rational decision-making process. Scientists tell us the response originates in the limbic system of the brain, which is the seat of our emotions. Roger Seymour, a psychologist in Alta Loma, California, describes this system's limited function: "The limbic system's vocabulary is composed of a few hundred signals," he notes. Those signals aren't words or coherent thoughts, but emotions such as fear, joy, relief, or dread. By contrast, he explains, "The prefrontal cortex has an almost unlimited vocabulary." And this is the part of our brains that we use to analyze, plan, distinguish right from wrong, and interact socially.

Within the limbic system is a small structure known as the amygdala, which controls our response to emergencies. "It has a vocabulary of two," Seymour says. "The amygdala is the part of the brain that stores wordless terror, or, *everything's okay.*" In other words, it's concerned with the basic issues of life and death. It is one of few areas of the brain that are fully developed at birth, which suggests its function is critical to our survival. This also means that we can experience terror before we have the capacity to understand it; the parts of our brain that might help us *explain* frightening events are not yet fully developed. So, when something happens which dredges up that childhood terror and triggers the amygdala's panic response, all our rational tools are useless. A cascade of hormones is released in our bodies, preparing us to act aggressively before we have a chance to mull things over. And that's why in a crisis we do things that don't seem to make sense.

The perceived threat may be something obvious, such as a physical attack or an impending car wreck. But it can also be something far more subtle: Arguments, threatening words, or fear of imminent loss can trigger this reaction as quickly as an attacking predator. The familiar sound of a belligerent voice can send us into emergency mode. Receiving an ominous letter in the mail can induce an irrational state of panic.

And our responses may not be the obvious ones of physically fighting or running. When we raise our voices in defiance, or refuse to concede even a trivial point in an argument, that can be an expression of the *fight* reflex. Retreating into another room, refusing to communicate, or escaping into some addictive behavior can be a form of *fleeing*, or running away. Likewise, when our eyes glaze over and we find ourselves suddenly unable to act, that can be a manifestation of the *freeze* response.

While these internal upheavals are driving our behavior, the last thing we should be doing is making long-term decisions involving huge amounts of money. But that's exactly what happens in many divorce situations. I've already described how clients often run away and stop communicating during the sale of their property. This is a flight response, as surely as if they were being chased by a bear. But this action doesn't help matters and only hinders a process that must go forward. And some ex-partners will fight over silly things on principle, even when it hurts them. I've watched clients go into court with their lawyers and haggle over who should keep the candlesticks and napkin rings! Of course, they paid thousands of dollars for that privilege.

In one memorable example from my practice, a divorcing partner was willing to destroy his whole life just to strike a final blow against his ex-wife. Brad owned a commercial building from which he operated a successful business. He and his wife, Shirley, also owned a second house, which they rented out. When they divorced, it was agreed that he would keep the commercial building and his business; she would get the rental. It was a fair arrangement, since the equity in both properties was about equal. But then Brad convinced a friend to file a $200,000 lien on the rental property—just so Shirley couldn't access the equity. Their case was under the court's jurisdiction, and the judge was not pleased. He ordered Brad to have the lien removed and threatened to force a sale of the commercial property to give Shirley the money she was entitled to. Brad responded by filing bankruptcy. But that only stalled the process; it couldn't halt it. After much legal maneuvering, Brad's commercial property was removed from the bankruptcy proceeding and sold out from under him. He lost his marriage, his property, his reputation, his business, his fortune, and ten years of his life—just to satisfy a mad desire for revenge.

That was a dramatic example of the irrational behavior that may be spawned by divorce. But not all cases are so extreme. Some have a façade of reasonableness, but the substance is the same. Kristen was a client who called me when her divorce was pending, asking me to help sell her house. She warned me about her husband, Jim: "He's going to be very uncooperative," she said. "You'll need to be careful!" As it turned out, Jim was perfectly reasonable, but Kristen actually dug in her heels when the time came to strike a deal. A solid offer came in on their house, which would have allowed each of them to walk away with more than $100,000. That wasn't good enough for Kristen. She insisted on submitting several counteroffers, each one disputing trivial aspects of the deal. She wouldn't take yes for an answer! It soon became apparent that the sale was a metaphor for her battle with Jim. And she had to win.

These are responses I've learned to expect, especially in high-conflict divorces. My role as a real estate agent is to cool things down and recommend solutions that will be most beneficial to the clients. When I'm appointed by a court to oversee the sale of a home, I am a neutral body. My only client is whoever is on the title to the property. I have to be unbiased regarding the spousal conflict—and I must appear that way too. That means giving each partner equal attention, recognition, validation, and eye contact. In Kristen's case, my first impulse was to rebut her unreasonable demands one by one. Instead, I opted for a more empathic approach, hoping to defuse her anger. After years of dealing with hostile and belligerent people, I've learned that most are being driven by fear—that wordless terror that even they may not understand. With these folks it doesn't help to make well-reasoned arguments. They need to be heard, reassured, and then guided toward a solution in their best interests.

Getting Help

If it's hazardous to make big decisions during the emotional roller coaster of divorce, what's the answer? Aren't some decisions forced on us at this very vulnerable time? Indeed, they are. Fortunately, there are experts whose calling is to help us make those decisions and get through the crisis intact. An attorney is often the first phone call for people facing a divorce, and rightly so. But the lawyer's job is limited to completing the divorce under the best conditions possible for the client. Even the best lawyer can't address the many other issues that a breakup involves. Mark Baer, an attorney in Pasadena, California, who works mainly in family law, sees this dilemma up close: "We might be able to listen to the clients and be empathic to them," he says. "But where is our training in dealing with emotions? There is none." The same could be said regarding the financial, credit, career, and relationship aspects of a breakup.

That's where other experts can play a vital role. As I've mentioned, I interact regularly with a network of professionals from various disciplines: attorneys, mediators, therapists, child psychologists, financial advisors, and credit experts. Their services complement each other, and help their clients emerge from divorce with the least amount of damage. These professionals can act as a buffer, protecting clients from their own worst impulses in times of emotional distress.

The key is to seek help proactively—before the horse is out of the barn, as it were. In my field, I've been privileged to help many clients navigate the real estate maze successfully. But I could have helped many more if they had come to me earlier in the process—*before* making those critical decisions. The other professionals I work with would undoubtedly say the same thing.

Doug Minor is a credit expert based in Sherman Oaks, California, who helps consumers repair their credit; he also testifies frequently as an expert witness. Many of his clients are people in the midst of divorce—or their attorneys, in cases that go to trial. He's well acquainted with the human tendency to act impulsively out of fear, and he often has to help clients pick up the pieces afterward. Here's how he describes the ones who come to him after making a mess of things: "They're a little bit anxious and fearful, and they read things online—and then they start doing whatever they read. It's a fear-based situation but it manifests itself in a hodgepodge of fixes." In repairing credit damage, Minor points out, it's important not just to do the right things—but to do them in the right sequence. He often finds himself repairing damage that clients have done to themselves by acting impulsively without good advice.

Loan underwriter Denise Fontyn sees a similar dynamic with people who are seeking financing in the context of a divorce. If she can get to them before they make the big decisions, her chances of helping them are much better. When ex-partners are fighting, looking at the hard numbers can bring a certain calm: "The computation of what their options are brings the tension down," she says. "They're realizing that it's not worth fighting over. The guy that wants to stay and buy his wife out, when he realizes he can't afford the mortgage payments, he stops pushing for that option. Or, when they realize that there's no equity, 'What are we fighting over the house for? It's upside down $150,000! You want it? Here you go, you can have it!'" At such times, hearing commonsense advice from an objective source is invaluable.

Many divorcing spouses would welcome the presence of a personal counselor just to help them get through the process. As it happens, such people exist; they're called *divorce coaches*. Along with her practice as a marriage and family therapist, Joyce Tessier specializes as a collaborative divorce and mediation coach in Orange County, California. She describes that role in "The Emotional Divorce":

> The primary function of coaching is to create a context in which life and performance enhancement may take place. Coaching assumes that the client is already functioning and is capable of taking directed action to accomplish what they perceive as success.
>
> Coaching works in the gap between the present and the post-divorce future. In coaching, history is approached only as the map that brought the client to the present.

Throughout the process, a coach will assist the client to foster a sense of control; defuse their fear of the separation/divorce process; structure information gathering; help them to organize their basic living tasks during this time of confusion and emotional upheaval.

With such help, the financial and logistical challenges of divorce become more manageable. You can avoid the trap of making impulsive decisions based on emotions that are out of control. Knowing that your decision-making capacity is not at its best can actually lead to a sense of relief: You realize that you don't have to go it alone, and so can set about getting the help you need.

CHAPTER SIX

Considering the Kids

If you have children, their welfare will naturally weigh heavily in your decision-making, as it should. But we've noted that knee-jerk decisions made "for the kids" aren't always the best. On the other hand, you may be so overwhelmed by your own emotional crises that the kids become a distant afterthought. Some clearheaded guidance will help you avoid both pitfalls.

Even while you're trying to do what's best for your children, what happens to the house may ultimately be beyond your control; if you can't afford to stay in any plausible scenario, your decision is made for you. You will be finding a new home, and your challenge then is to make the transition as trauma-free as possible.

But often, things are not that clear-cut. Sometimes one partner could afford to keep the home, but doesn't want to. The other spouse must determine whether staying is an option, and if so, whether it's really worth it. Finances are often the determining factor in that choice. If staying means consigning the family to a life of poverty, moving may be the better option.

Sadly, today's legal environment doesn't always help spouses in this situation. In the past, it was very common for a divorcing wife to keep the family home to provide a stable environment for the children. Since men were presumed to be the primary breadwinners, courts would require them to provide spousal and child support to help accomplish this goal. But in recent years that model has been largely abandoned.

Richard Hughes is a former court commissioner (one who serves under the general direction of the Presiding Judge performing various judicial functions) who recently retired after several decades on the bench in Southern California. His description of today's legal system would surprise many people. "Seldom does the house stay with the mother, like in the old days," he observes. "Usually, the mother has to move." There is no longer an automatic presumption that a mother should receive financial support. And for many women, keeping the house without that support is financially impossible. Ironically, the remarkable achievements of women in the workplace can work against them when they enter a divorce court. Hughes describes the ethos that prevails now: "The mother has to work, just like the father works."

Sometimes the court's decisions on support issues do not even involve human input. In California, for example, child and spousal support is calculated by a software program called the DissoMaster. As Hughes describes, the directives that emerge from this impersonal system can come as a shock:

You have somebody who is a computer engineer, who is a mother, and she's twenty-eight years old. And she leaves the workforce to take care of her two- and three-year-old children; the DissoMaster will say, "You have to go to work, and if you don't go to work, we're going to ascribe the salary you would get if you had gone to work." So she's really in trouble. That forces her to go back into the workforce.

It can also force her out of her home, as an unintended

consequence. Hughes sums up the unhappy state of affairs: "The courts—the law—have no sympathy for the mother."

When Staying Is the Right Choice

If you can get past these legal and practical obstacles, you may have the luxury of deciding on your own whether to keep the family home. And all other things being equal, it *may* be best for the children to stay in their familiar environment. Ann Bingham Newman is a psychologist in California who works with children of divorce. "Home is a sacred place for kids," she notes. "It's where the family is, it's where all the good things happen, where their toys are, where their animals are. It's familiar. They know where to go and hide. Even if there's a lot of conflict and tension, I think it's still their sanctuary." But as we've discussed, you shouldn't presume to know what will benefit the children without taking a careful reading of their feelings and attitudes. Communication is never more important than at this critical phase of your family's journey.

A story I heard while attending a seminar illustrates the point well: Jimmy's parents were divorcing but were very earnest about keeping his life as normal as possible in the meantime. They were sharing custody and arranged for little Jimmy to have identical accommodations at both houses: the same bedding, the same room color, duplicates of all his important possessions. But after Jimmy talked with a child psychologist, the parents were stunned to learn what his real concerns were: His number one fear was that now Dad wouldn't be able to take him to get bagels on the way to school, which had become their daily practice. That mundane routine was the most comforting thing in his life, and in all their good intentions his parents could easily have missed it.

Keeping the Door Open

Dr. Bingham Newman offers this candid advice for divorcing parents: "You have to keep that door or window open; you have to communicate with kids! And if you haven't been up till then, you'd better start." She provides a printed handout (that she shares below) for divorcing parents to help them in this endeavor. Among its suggestions:

1. Tell your child as soon as a definite decision is reached.

2. Make sure all family members (including both parents) are present.

3. Plan ahead about exactly when and what you are going to say.

4. Be honest and straightforward.

5. Give a simple reason for the divorce.

6. Don't assess blame.

7. Emphasize that your child did not cause the divorce.

8. Emphasize that both parents will continue to love and care for the child.

9. Emphasize that your child is still part of a family.

10. Describe things that will stay the same.

11. Describe changes that will occur.

12. If your child is older, outline steps that have been taken to save the marriage.

13. Acknowledge your child's feelings.

14. Encourage questions.

15. Repeat the information on more than one occasion.

Most of us acknowledge the importance of communication but find it difficult to practice—especially with our children. Put simply, they don't often say what they're really feeling. As Dr. Bingham Newman observes, "They're more likely to tell the parents what they think the parent wants to hear." To get the true picture, we must use our eyes as well as our ears. "You can sometimes discern it from watching their behavior," she says, "because their behavior speaks very loudly." While they may not verbalize their experiences, "silence *doesn't* mean everything is okay."

And remember, she says, each child is different: "You have to know your kids." Some are easygoing and cope more readily with change. Others harbor hidden insecurities that are easy to miss. She recalls one child who moved to a new home after a divorce and was extremely disturbed when a drunken neighbor inadvertently knocked down the mailbox. To the child, that mailbox represented a sense of order in what had become a very chaotic world. He felt compelled to restore that little piece of normalcy. Bingham Newman recalls, "He got a little box and wrote on it, *Mailman, put mail here.*" The mail carrier was probably amused but surely had no idea of the deep motivations behind that childish act.

These issues are on my radar every day because of the work I do; I live and breathe the divorce environment, so I'm very aware of how parents can hurt their children. I always thought I had a pretty good line of communication with my own kids, but as I found out, even a conscientious parent can get it wrong.

We sent our oldest son to summer camp one year, and he loved it. When we picked him up afterward, he was elated. But when we sent him again the next year, his reaction was the opposite; he seemed almost dejected when we picked him up, and I couldn't figure out why. I told myself that the initial excitement had probably just worn off. But as a parent, I found the worst possible scenarios rolling through my imagination.

Much later, our nanny told me the real reason: "You know," she said, "when Andrew came home from camp he went up to his room and he cried." She had gone up to see him and was surprised when he pulled out a stash of papers he had been keeping. As he showed them to her, she was even more surprised to realize what they were: all the letters I had written to him at camp the year before! They meant so much to him that he had kept them. And this year, there hadn't been any.

There were good reasons for my lapse: It was an exceptionally busy time for our family. On top of my business activities, we were in the process of moving. That meant managing two complicated sales transactions at once. At the same time, we were preparing for a trip to Florida. In the rush of activity, I simply never got around to writing to my son. And I was oblivious to the effect that had on him. For someone who should know these things, I had messed up big time!

When Andrew finally broke the ice, he didn't let me off the hook easy. "You never wrote to me, Mom!" he scolded. "All the other kids got something and I didn't; I waited every day, and you never wrote to me!" Needless to say, the next year I changed my ways. He was excited about going to camp again, and after sending him off with a promise that I wouldn't forget this time, I wrote him a nice letter—complete with a picture of our family dog.

The lesson is that kids don't always tell us what's bothering them. And they can be amazingly sensitive to little things that we might overlook. Combine that with the extraordinary trauma of divorce, and the potential for real damage is sobering.

When Leaving Becomes Imperative

There is one situation in which selling the home is likely the right thing to do, regardless of the financial circumstances. Dr. Bingham Newman recalls a young patient who had to witness horrific scenes of violence in the family home, night after night. "The child watched that from behind the stairway," she says. "He would sneak down and watch Dad throttling Mom. In that instance, I think it's better to get out of that house; remove everybody."

Such environments can produce lasting damage in children. Ongoing traumatic events may cause bright kids to behave as if they were mentally impaired, or it may even disrupt their physical development—causing a condition known as *psychosocial dwarfism*. Staying in the home where abuse occurred can force a child to relive those memories, and no comfortable dwelling is worth that price. In such circumstances, you and your children will be better off living somewhere else.

The Balancing Act

In making these decisions, you must weigh several factors and determine what is most important. We've discussed the financial deprivation that some families experience when they opt to keep the house at all costs. And as Dr. Bingham Newman observes, it's hard to hide these things from the children. "Financial stress is big for kids," she notes. "They pick it up. You don't even have to talk about it, because they hear you maybe say things like, 'Well, we can't get that today because we don't have enough money.'" As a result, many children come to view themselves as the cause of stress and feel guilty—even though it's not their fault.

As much as she favors keeping a familiar environment for

children, Dr. Bingham Newman acknowledges that there are times when it's not worth it. Among other factors, she points out, poverty is a major cause of poor academic performance. "If they're going to be impoverished, and they aren't going to have clothes, and they aren't going to be able to eat right or go to the dentist—all those little things that you sort of take for granted—then move," she urges. "You need to have enough money."

Smoothing the Transition

There are ways to lessen the impact that a move has on the children. One is to bring the changes on slowly—in stages. The first shock for kids, obviously, is that Mom or Dad is leaving. If you don't have to move immediately, consider giving them time and space to process that change. Then at the right time, gently introduce the idea of moving.

Remember the list of guidelines we mentioned earlier? At this stage, it's important to observe number ten: *Describe things that will stay the same.* You may need to use your imagination, and keep in mind that little things can be important. In the first phase, when Dad or Mom has recently left, reassure the kids that many things will remain as before. Dr. Bingham Newman illustrates how you might approach this:

> "We'll be staying in the same house; Grandma will be two blocks away. You can still ride your bike to school; it's only two blocks—you can see it. And, your friends are right around there. You can still have play dates, and things like that at our house." So, the more things can stay the same, even if it's, say, for three months or six months, it's better.

Then, when moving time comes, continue to preserve as many familiar things as possible:

> You try to make sure they can bring something with them that's the same, something similar; that they can pick out colors for their room. They can even help paint, they can help box things up, they can have their own little box that they put their stuff in—anything that involves them in the process is always helpful.

Meanwhile, the *way* you communicate to the children is all-important. It's okay to be straightforward and honest—even to cry. The kids know this is a big deal, after all. It would be odd to them if you didn't react emotionally! But you can also be positive, reassuring them that you'll always be there. The last thing they need to see is Mom or Dad quaking in fear. As Dr. Bingham Newman notes, this can send them into a panic response: "All the cortisol goes right into their brains and we have the *fight, flight or freeze* [reaction]—and they freeze. And the only thing that's working is their emotional brain; their cognitive brain has been put aside. They can't concentrate; they can't do anything in school." You can be real, vulnerable, and human—but still be strong. That's what your kids need.

In explaining the reasons for moving, simply say that Mom and Dad make a certain amount of money, and now that income needs to pay for two households instead of one. So, that means moving to a less-expensive home. They'll still have their own beds, their toys, and favorite possessions. And things will be okay. With a little effort, you can even make it fun. Are you looking at a number of prospective homes? Include the kids in that process. You can say, for example, "I've found three places, guys, and I need your help picking one! This complex over here has a community swimming pool, and there's a barbecue. The other one is near a beautiful park . . ."

You may also need to monitor how you speak about your ex-spouse. Remember, children view themselves as 50 percent Mom and 50 percent Dad. When you criticize the other parent, they can easily internalize that, thinking—perhaps unconsciously—*Mom (or Dad) is really saying that about me.* Needless to say, that can mess them up in a big way. And how much worse if both parents are doing it! Be careful also in the way you speak to other people when you don't think the kids are listening. They may overhear your conversations with family or friends, and your offhand comments can be just as destructive as a deliberate smear campaign.

In this time of transition, engaging a child therapist can be invaluable. In her practice, Ann Bingham Newman manages to elicit honest responses from kids by providing a safe place for them to express themselves. "I have a playroom," she says. "They come in the playroom and they go, 'Oh, wow!' And they don't want to go home. And they feel very comfortable, and they can talk, and they can play. And they play out whatever's going on. So I usually find out more than anybody."

Another helpful step: Take a co-parenting class with your ex. You'll learn how to talk with each other, perhaps as you never did before. And importantly, you'll learn how to avoid putting the children in the middle of your conflict.

Finally, as you move toward this new phase of your life, you may need to remind yourself what you've been telling your kids: *We're going to be okay!*

With good information and the right attitude, you will.

CHAPTER SEVEN

When There's No Equity to Divide

Not long ago I received a call from a local attorney who was handling a divorce case. She said the court had appointed me to handle the sale of John and Brenda's residence. They owed about $530,000 on their mortgage but figured the property was worth at least $700,000. They had also invested over $100,000 in upgrades, so they felt confident that they'd get their price and come out with plenty of money for each spouse.

Unfortunately, this occurred during a declining market, and the recent comparable sales told a different story. My research revealed that the fair market value was closer to $550,000. Their unrealistic figure was the result of a common misjudgment. As we've pointed out, people often base their guesses of value on unreliable information: the asking prices of nearby homes, neighborhood rumors, or sales long past. When they see the real numbers, it can hit like a slap in the face.

The discrepancy in value figures was just the first sign of trouble for John and Brenda. Their loan was one of the infamous "pick-a-pay" loans that became popular during the real estate boom of the early twenty-first century. These instruments allowed borrowers to choose from several repayment plans, with the "easiest" ones incurring *negative amortization*—that is, the borrowers owed more each month rather than less. As you guessed, that was the option my clients had chosen, so after two years in the home their unpaid balance was actually $549,000.

It got worse. Their loan had not provided an impound, or escrow, account for taxes and insurance, so we discovered they owed $12,000 in unpaid property taxes. To top it all off, their loan stipulated a prepayment penalty, so if they sold before three years in the home they would owe the bank another six months' interest. I knew that local home values were dropping fast, so just before delivering this bad news, I did another market analysis. I learned that three new foreclosures nearby had skewed the prices downward again. The home had lost another $50,000 in value—in just one week.

What they had assumed was a comfortable equity sale with substantial proceeds for everyone suddenly became very complicated. There would be no money for either of the divorcing spouses—or for the attorneys, who were counting on the proceeds to cover their fees. It was now clear that we were looking at a short sale. That meant asking the mortgage company to accept whatever the sale proceeds were as full payment of the loan.

Short sales can be a nightmare—and a saving grace. Although they are maddeningly complex, they provide welcome relief for those who need them. They became common in the wake of the housing crisis as rising mortgage defaults led to a full-fledged recession, and property values in some areas plunged by as much as half. Since then the market has improved, and many homeowners have regained equity. But short sales are still common—especially in regions hit hardest by the housing crash—and will probably remain so for some time. For those who obtained their financing at the peak of the market, positive equity may be years away. But they still might need to liquidate their loans, for any number of reasons. Beyond the divorce scenario, borrowers may experience loss of employment, sickness, the death of a breadwinner, or a job transfer. In these cases, a short sale is often the only good option. It's usually the best option for the mortgage holders (banks) as well: They dispose of a problem loan without the time and expense of reclaiming the property, marketing it as an REO (bank-owned property), and maintaining it through the long foreclosure process.

But short sales are also perilous. And as anyone who has experienced one can testify, they, too, can take months or years to complete. That leads many distressed homeowners—and real estate agents—to shy away from them. Divorcing homeowners often feel that they simply can't handle one more stressful thing, and short sales are definitely stressful. So they resign themselves to foreclosure: *Everything else has fallen apart; might as well just let the house go, too. How could it make things any worse?*

This is an understandable sentiment. But as we've discussed, making big decisions in the midst of emotional turmoil is a recipe for disaster. And most people don't fully realize that a foreclosure can deeply hurt their financial prospects for years. In these situations, the best option may be to hand the whole thing over to a professional who is experienced in the process and unconnected to it emotionally. The professional does the work and bears the stress so you can refocus on other pressing issues. Since there are no proceeds to fight over, you literally have nothing to lose in the short term. And in the long term, working with a skilled professional can position you to recover financially much faster than you might imagine.

In this regard, timing is critical. Many distressed homeowners realize that a short sale is probably inevitable, but they choose to put it off. They may hope that rising home values will make it unnecessary, or they may simply prefer not to think about it. But it's important to think strategically, with the long term in mind. How fast can you realistically expect the home values to rise in your neighborhood? And at that rate, how long will it take before you recover a positive equity position? To answer that question, you must have precise numbers on your home's current value and on how much you owe. Your most recent mortgage statement will indicate your unpaid balance at the time of the statement. But the actual payoff amount changes from day to day, and may include a range of charges that don't appear on the statement. Your agent can request a precise payoff figure from the mortgage company, which may take from a day to a week to obtain. Once you've estimated how long it will take to regain positive equity, the next question may be the hardest: Are you prepared to wait that long—just to break even?

Beyond the wasted time, there's also a very real risk in waiting: Your short sale may damage your credit profile at the very moment when you're trying to rebuild it. It may be better to take the hit early—while your scores are probably down anyway —and then let the recovery begin. That can start as soon as your short sale closes, so putting it off only delays the rebuilding process.

The Upside

The most obvious benefit of a short sale is that it allows you to escape an unsustainable mortgage. That can be an enormous relief when you've been struggling to make those monthly payments, or if you're underwater with no hope of regaining equity for years. You can start afresh, perhaps in a home that costs much less. In some cases, you can even make lease-back arrangements with the buyer, allowing you to remain in your home while shedding the unbearable burden of debt. Having a short sale on your record will damage your credit profile, but usually less than a foreclosure would. You may also be eligible to buy again much sooner than if you had simply resigned yourself to foreclosure.

A short sale also allows you to move out of your home in an orderly, dignified way, rather than being forced to leave on someone else's terms. The eviction process that follows foreclosure is traumatic and degrading. You could come home to find notices posted on your front door, the locks changed, or a sheriff's deputy waiting to escort you out! With a short sale you'll exit according to a predictable, mutually agreed timetable.

The Downside

There are also potential disadvantages to a short sale, which fall mainly into three categories: *credit damage, tax liability*, and remaining *debt liability*.

We've already mentioned the credit damage, which can be substantial.

The tax liability is something many people are unprepared for. When a debt is canceled, as in a foreclosure or a short sale, the creditor typically issues a 1099-C (*C* for *canceled*), which is also sent to the IRS. The forgiven amount is then considered taxable income. So at a time of maximum vulnerability, borrowers may find themselves on the hook for huge unanticipated tax bills. This is precisely what millions of borrowers were facing as the recent mortgage crisis got worse and worse. Congress recognized the extent of the problem and passed the Mortgage Forgiveness Debt Relief Act of 2007, exempting some, but not all, forgiven mortgage debt from federal income tax. The law was subsequently renewed, but expired at the end of 2013. In California, the IRS redefined the way that it qualified anti-deficiency, and conformed to California's Civil Code Section 580e, in which most short sales are anti-deficient. This is excellent news for California homeowners, but if the property is in a different state, I strongly encourage you to investigate your state's laws.

You may be able to find relief in another section of the tax code, regardless of what state in which the property is located. If you were *insolvent* at the time of your debt forgiveness, you may be exempt from taxation. Here's how the IRS describes its insolvency provision:

> The forgiven debt may qualify under the insolvency exclusion. Normally, you are not required to include forgiven debts in income to the extent that you are insolvent. You are insolvent when your total liabilities exceed your total assets. The forgiven debt may also qualify for exclusion if the debt was discharged in a Title 11 bankruptcy proceeding or if the debt is qualified farm indebtedness or qualified real property business indebtedness.

This covers tax liability at the federal level, but many states have their own income tax, which may have different requirements. Be sure to consult a tax professional regarding the impact of forgiven debt on your state income tax liability.

Even when mortgage companies agree to a short sale, it doesn't automatically mean the unpaid debt is forgiven. Some loans are *recourse loans*, meaning that the creditor can continue to pursue unpaid amounts after a foreclosure. As we've noted, the creditor may go to court and secure a *deficiency judgment*, and then try to collect the money in a number of ways, such as by attaching assets or garnishing wages. This can be a cruel surprise for those who thought their short sale (or foreclosure) would mark the end of their problems. It's essential to become familiar with the laws in your state. Some states are known as *non-recourse* states, meaning that if a creditor forecloses it is prohibited from pursuing further collection activities. But even then, the laws may only apply to certain types of loans (such as purchase-money loans on principal residences). Before committing to a permanent course of action, investigate the laws in your state and their potential ramifications for you. A skilled attorney, Realtor, or financial advisor can be invaluable in this regard.

As always, things become more complex when there is more than one loan on a property: One may be a recourse loan; another, non-recourse. Many homeowners have a home equity line of credit in addition to their first mortgage. These can be recourse loans that are attached to the person as well as the property—like a credit card secured by the home. This means that although a short sale or foreclosure may erase the lien, the borrower will still have an obligation to pay. In such cases, a short sale offers a unique opportunity to negotiate the terms of settlement. In the short sale process, all creditors with an interest in the property are brought to the bargaining table. A skilled agent may be able to achieve *full satisfaction* of the loan—releasing you from all liability—for a fraction of the unpaid balance.

Avoiding Surprises

Before making any long-range plans, it's important to find out whether your home has any equity. As we saw in the case study that begins this chapter, reality can pack some rude surprises. If you're envisioning a comfortable future based on imagined proceeds that will never actually materialize, it's better to find this out and make the adjustment now, rather than after the agreements have been signed and reality is knocking on your door.

In chapter 4, "What's Your House Worth, Anyway," we described how to obtain a realistic sale price for your property. Another important step before putting your house on the market is to run a title search, which your real estate agent can do for you. This will reveal any liens attached to the property and help you determine how much money you might receive after a sale. If the numbers point toward a short sale, your agent can then reach out to the respective creditors and begin negotiating the most favorable terms.

Here are some of the items that could be subtracted from your sale proceeds:

1. Unpaid balance on second mortgages

2. Home equity lines of credit (HELOCs)

3. Unpaid property taxes

4. IRS liens

5. Mechanic's liens (for unpaid construction or remodeling work)

6. Child support liens

7. Family law attorney's real property liens (FLARPLs)

8. Prepayment penalty riders

9. Unpaid homeowners association dues

10. Real estate sales commissions

11. Title and escrow fees

12. Termite damage repair costs

13. Other lender-mandated repairs

By estimating these costs, adding them up, and subtracting the total from your expected sale price, you'll get an idea whether you're looking at a short sale—or if you can expect some money at the end of it all.

Getting Approval

For a short sale to proceed, every affected stakeholder must approve it: all the mortgage holders as well as any other lien holders. Many loans have *mortgage insurance* (MI), which must also be taken into account. When the mortgage holder takes a loss on a loan, it will file a claim against this insurance policy, so the insurance company must agree with the terms of the sale. Sometimes, the terms of the MI policy itself make it more advantageous for the mortgage holder to foreclose on the property rather than agree to a short sale. These are some of the variables your real estate agent must wrestle with to chart a successful course for you.

If all this sounds complicated, it gets even more so: Many mortgage loans today are bundled into groups and sold as *mortgage-backed securities* (MBS), also known as *collateralized debt obligations* (CDOs). These securitized instruments are often covered by *pool insurance*—policies attached to the entire group rather than individual loans. Where this type of policy exists, it must be included in the short sale negotiations just like normal mortgage insurance. But the presence of this insurance may not be immediately evident, even to the servicer of the loan. Determining that will require extensive investigation to avoid last-minute surprises.

Behind the Curtain

Sometimes all the right elements are in place for a short sale and the bank still won't issue an approval. This has been the experience of many homeowners in recent years. They provide all the correct documentation and jump through all the hoops. It seems obvious that the transaction is in the bank's interests as well as the homeowner's—but the sale is declined. At that point, both homeowners and agents may throw up their hands in exasperation: *What is wrong with these people? Don't they get it?*

Usually, there's more going on in these situations than meets the eye. The loan servicer may be acting according to hidden agreements with the loan investors, or with the MI company as we discussed earlier. You won't be privy to these arrangements but will feel their effects. Rest assured that mortgage servicers are always looking at bottom-line numbers and making decisions that reflect their interests. It's up to you and your agent to protect yours.

Working with Buyers

Because short sales typically take a long time to complete, buyers sometimes become discouraged and drop out. To avoid this, your listing agent must maintain good communication with the buyer's agent throughout the process. It's also wise to screen potential buyers not just for their ability to buy, but for their commitment. They must be informed that the process can be arduous, and be prepared to stick it out. Some buyers make offers on multiple properties, hoping that one of them will work out. They have no real commitment to any particular home. If you find yourself dealing with such a buyer, consider well whether it's worth the risk. There may be more reliable buyers waiting in the wings.

Pressing Through

As you can see, a short sale is not for the fainthearted. But it can be worth the aggravation if it frees you from a huge debt burden and allows you to make a fresh start. And, as with any home sale, most of the burden is borne by your listing agent, freeing you to concentrate on other things. The key is to find a qualified short sale agent—one with training *and* experience— who has a track record of success. My own team is relentless and skilled when negotiating shorts sales, with a 96 percent short sale approval ratio compared with the industry average of about 50 percent. I say this to illustrate that while this is an extremely complicated area of real estate, it is not impossible to navigate and there are many real estate agents who succeed in the short sale sphere. Find one in your area, and you'll have a good chance at succeeding.

CHAPTER EIGHT

In the Courtroom

Most divorces never go to trial. In about 95 percent of cases the parties settle, their agreement is accepted by the court, and they go their separate way without having to spend time in a courtroom. But sometimes a trial is inevitable. There can be good reasons to contest a divorce. And there are always things to watch out for if you do.

Reasons to Go to Trial

If you and your soon-to-be ex simply can't agree on important issues, the courtroom is a valid place to resolve them. Usually those issues concern one of two areas: the division of material asset, or child custody. Attorney Pamela Edwards-Swift describes some of the things that drive people into court: "It could be the issue of the value of the business, or maybe the spousal support; is there going to be spousal support? If so, how much? And what's the length or the duration going to be? What are we doing with the kids? All of those things can be an issue; it just depends on where you can agree or not agree."

Pension funds and investment accounts can be major points of contention, especially if they're worth a lot. But in most cases, the main asset is the marital home. We've discussed the dangers that can arise in that area and the common misconceptions that can lead to costly mistakes. Those risks are amplified when a case goes to trial, because the decisions are out of both parties' hands. The court will decide how the assets are divided. Court judgments can be appealed, but that costs more time and money. And in the meantime, the court's rulings must be observed.

On the other hand, the power of the court can work to your advantage if you're the weaker party: A judge can simply order your ex to do things he or she would never voluntarily agree to. And the court can compel parties to hand over information they may prefer to withhold, such as the value of stock portfolios or pension funds. In such cases, going to court can level the playing field. But there's a price to pay for those advantages.

Time

By now it should be clear that even in the best of circumstances, your divorce will take several months if not years. And that time is greatly extended if you go to trial. How long will it take, from beginning to end? Family law specialist Pamela Edwards-Swift paints a sobering picture:

It could be within a year of filing a petition; it could be within three years or more of filing the petition. It really depends on the court we're in. You may see the judge on other issues: child support, child custody, and spousal support. You may see the judge on other things. But in terms of the actual trial date, yeah, it's going to take anywhere between a year and three years.

Before your trial even begins you'll be making multiple court appearances, often for just a few minutes at a time, to address specific issues. Both attorneys will likely file discovery motions, demanding all pertinent information about the case from the other side. This in itself can involve considerable haggling, which in turn consumes more time, both in court and out. While you're awaiting your trial, the court will need to address short-term practical matters such as who keeps the children, who gets to live in the house, and who makes the payments.

When a pressing issue is not resolved or a new one arises, it usually becomes necessary to schedule another appearance at a later date. And if the attorneys find that they need more time to prepare, they can ask for a continuance or adjournment, further delaying the proceedings. These requests are routinely granted, especially the first time. If a lawyer asks for such postponements repeatedly, it can be a sign of inattention or incompetence—frustrating enough when it's the opposing attorney, but especially so when it's your attorney.

All of this is subject to the court calendar, which is probably overloaded already, so you may go weeks or months between appearances. And even when your court date finally arrives, you'll spend a lot of time sitting and waiting. Typically, your case will be one of several on the docket, and the other cases may take longer than expected. You might be scheduled for 9 a.m. but not come before the judge until noon—or even after lunch. If you need to take time off from work for each appearance, the process can become very inconvenient very quickly. It's easy to see why divorces can drag on for years! Meanwhile, much of your life is on hold. You'll find it hard to buy a new home or to refinance the old one until the divorce is final; with so many unresolved variables, a lender will have no basis for assessing your ability to repay a loan.

Money

Needless to say, the attorneys expect to be paid for all those court appearances as well as the time they spend consulting, researching, preparing motions, and writing letters. If they're being paid hourly, the meter normally starts running from the time they leave the office to go to the courthouse. And it continues running while they're waiting for the case to be called, for witnesses to appear, for the other attorney to make arguments, and for the judge to make a decision.

Only you can decide whether your eventual reward will be worth the time and expense of a trial. In making that decision, balance your passion with cold-eyed realism. And make sure you understand the pitfalls you're likely to encounter. Attorney Mark Baer identifies the main risk in going to trial: "You can't predict what a judge will do," he says. "You don't know for sure what the result is going to be." Only one result is virtually certain, according to Baer: "You're not going to see two people walking out of the courtroom happy. You're either going to see one person happy and one person unhappy, or you're going to see two people unhappy."

Richard Vogl is a retired commissioner in the Superior Court in Santa Ana, California, who now volunteers for legal aid programs. During his career of over forty years he observed a wide range of human motivations in the courtroom setting:

> You may have a situation where everybody's taking a position and they're not going to budge and you get the attorneys involved and the attorneys can either help you reach agreement, or they can litigate. And every case is different, depending on the personalities of the parties and/or the attorneys.

As Vogl notes, it's not always the divorcing parties that drive the process:

You may have the parties that want to resolve the cases but maybe their attorneys do not, for whatever reason. So the case takes on the personalities of the attorneys.

And sometimes litigants are motivated by an unreasonable desire for vengeance:

You may have a person [who says], "I know that it's going to cost me $100,000 to collect $110,000 or $90,000, but I don't care. It's the principle of the thing. I want to do it." It's because they've been wronged in some way, or they feel they've been wronged. So now they're going to make the other side pay.

To Err Is Human

Attorneys and judges are only human. They make mistakes. Your case may be one of dozens that come before the court on a given day. Does the judge seem remote, jaded, gruff, or impatient? You might be too, if you had to watch an endless parade of human greed, squalor, and misery every day. Attorneys must deal with mountains of paperwork on each case they handle. It shouldn't be too surprising if some details are neglected or mishandled. Commissioner Vogl observes that this is especially common in cases involving divorce and real estate. Attorneys are often unprepared because they don't understand the intricacies of the real estate field. And, as Vogl notes, "Preparation is everything."

As an example, Vogl says, "When we talk about the mixing of community property assets and [other assets], you need to know: What was the value back then? What was the mortgage back then? What payments were made? What is the value of the money that went in? And, what are all the numbers now? And that proportion has to be worked out." Making such calculations may be beyond the abilities of most attorneys who were trained in law, not real estate finance. The easy thing to do then is to throw it back into the judge's lap. As Vogl says, "Lawyers come into court and say, 'Okay, here's all we know . . . You do it, your honor!" In such cases, Vogl didn't hesitate to throw it back, delaying a decision until the parties could come in with workable numbers. "I've had two witnesses where they couldn't even agree on the square footage of the house," he marvels. Needless to say, such disputes consume valuable time. As he observes, "Doing it right the first time is so important."

Decisions Regarding the House

With the exception of child custody issues, few decisions a court makes are as weighty as those regarding the marital home. In the blink of an eye, judgments can be rendered that will affect the rest of your life, and those of your children. But while the case is still in process, you have a chance to shape the outcome by mutual agreement. For example, you can agree that the home will be sold, and the court will generally go along with that. If one party violates that stipulation, the court may step in and order the agreement to be carried out. But as attorney Pamela Edwards-Swift observes, "Absent a stipulation, the court, as a general rule will not order a home to be sold unless there is a compelling reason to do so—such as an imminent foreclosure."

That gives great power to the divorcing parties during the initial phases—so long as they can cooperate with each other. This is a good time to heed the biblical admonition to "agree with your adversary quickly"—just not *too* quickly, or before seeking expert advice. The window for reaching a consensual arrangement will eventually close. Edwards-Swift describes the process:

> You file a petition for dissolution, and then the case goes along and eventually if you don't settle the case, you have a trial date. Now, at the time of trial they will order it sold. But they're not going to order it sold anytime between point A and point Z, unless there's a really good reason to do so.

Once that moment of judgment comes, it can be swift and unsparing. As Vogl says, "The duty of the court is to divide the community property. If the house is community property, the duty of the court is to divide it. The court has the power to allow one party to remain in it and order equivalent payment of the equity on a date certain." (This applies in California, which is a community property state; procedures in other states may vary, but the need to reach a judgment does not.) What happens if one party doesn't comply? "I see orders where the court says, 'Sir, you have ninety days to buy her out,'" Vogl says. "And then he gets the loan on the ninety-first day—now, what do we do?" Obviously, the resolution is delayed. "But if it's delayed," Vogl says, "there's going to be interest." The unpaid balance begins accruing interest charges from the first day of noncompliance. And as Vogl notes, "The court can't waive the interest—it's by law."

Sometimes courts issue rulings that are simply unworkable. A judge may agree with the divorcing spouses that the marital home should be sold and the proceeds divided. Financial arrangements may be based on a presumption that the home will fetch a certain price. But what if it doesn't receive any offers and has to be marked down? In another scenario, the parties may agree that one spouse will refinance the home and buy out the other party. But what if that person can't qualify for a loan? Courts often make misguided rulings in cases like this, because they aren't familiar with the realities of the market. And the attorneys may agree for the same reason. Such complications can throw the entire process into chaos, costing you time, money, and grief. It's your future that is on the line. Be proactive and protect yourself: Get a realistic property valuation beforehand; obtain that loan preapproval early on.

Representing Yourself

Nationwide, almost half of all family law litigants are pro per (also referred to as pro se), meaning they represent themselves in court. In the county where I practice, the number is closer to 80 percent. The main reason for this is economic: People simply can't afford to hire a lawyer. Predictably, this becomes more common in a sagging economy. While representing oneself is certainly an option, it carries obvious risks. Real estate matters are complex even without a divorce, and few untrained people can manage them without help. What's more, the legal process is virtually incomprehensible to a layperson. If you go into court pro per while your spouse is represented by an attorney, you're automatically at a severe disadvantage. There are low-cost alternatives: Most areas offer some form of free legal aid. And new attorneys sometimes take cases pro bono (for free) to gain experience, or they will take on certain aspects of your case, commonly known as unbundled legal services or under a limited scope retainer. Don't hesitate to explore the options in your area.

Eyes Wide Open

The court system exists to provide remedies for legitimate disputes. It can be your friend; it can also be a severe drain on your time, your resources, and your life. Be sure this is the route you really want before taking the plunge. And make sure you've explored the various alternatives first.

CHAPTER NINE

Peaceable Alternatives

A divorce doesn't have to be an all-out war. If a courtroom conflict doesn't appeal to you, there are other avenues to complete your divorce that can be easier on your emotions—and your checkbook. They can also be far quicker than going to court, which translates into less expense and less prolonged grief. Most important, they keep the decisions on important issues—such as the house—in your hands. In court, as we've discussed, divorcing parties surrender much of their power. The court has authority to make decisions that will be binding on you and your ex. And after spending a lot of time, money, and effort, you may not like the way things turn out.

The easiest solution is to have an uncontested divorce, which is the route most divorcing people choose. One party draws up a divorce petition—preferably with an attorney's help—and the other simply agrees. This may not be feasible when there are substantial assets or other issues involved that require deeper scrutiny and negotiation. And if one spouse is abusive or uncooperative, it may be impossible. But even when serious negotiations are unavoidable, there are ways to work out the thorny issues in a non-adversarial way—if both parties are willing.

Mediation

Mediation is one of the viable alternatives for people who want to avoid going to court. In this process the spouses select a neutral third party to facilitate an agreement that they can both live with. They meet with the mediator as often as necessary to hammer out arrangements regarding property, child custody, support, and all the other issues that must be resolved in a divorce agreement. If communication bogs down, the mediator's task is to bring the parties back together and refocus them on the task at hand.

Mediation offers a number of advantages over the adversarial approach:

1. It saves time. When you litigate your case in court, your progress is tied to the court's calendar, which almost guarantees a long timeline. When you finally get your day in court, it may be just the beginning of a seemingly endless ordeal. Each new issue may require a new court date and another long wait. These appearances often require the participation of all the parties. What if one doesn't show up in court? It's back to the calendar for another court date, and another delay. Meanwhile, the legal fees keep mounting—and your life is on hold. By contrast, mediation can proceed according to any schedule you agree on with your spouse and the mediator.

2. It's less expensive. The court process we've described can wind up costing both parties a lot of money. Beyond the court appearances, numerous other activities will rack up legal bills. The discovery process that accompanies litigated divorce—whereby the parties request and provide pertinent information to each other—can chew up substantial time and money all by itself. In mediation the time can be shortened considerably.

3. It's less emotionally draining. As we've seen, hurt feelings can drive people to do things that aren't in their best interests—such as quarrel over issues that really don't matter or pick fights they can't win. If your breakup has already been emotionally devastating, consider whether you really want to keep excavating those wounds. Mediation provides the chance to reach a reasonable conclusion without escalating to all-out war. Of course, the emotional toll is much greater when there are children involved. Choosing the more peaceable route can lessen their emotional trauma as well as your own.

4. It allows for open communication. When divorcing spouses retain attorneys, among the first things they're told is not to communicate directly with the other party. This is appropriate from the attorneys' point of view, but it may also prevent you from reaching agreements that might have been easily accomplished. Simple issues become complex and drag on needlessly. Mediation takes the opposite approach; even though attorneys may be involved, open and thorough communication between the parties is usually encouraged. When circumstances permit, it can be healthier and more expedient for you to speak up in your own behalf. It's your life, after all! And some issues are best resolved through frank discussion.

5. It's private. The mediation process and the resulting agreements are confidential and private. By contrast, court proceedings and transcripts are open to the public. This may not be a big issue for most people, but if you are a high-profile person or simply value your privacy, it's something to keep in mind.

6. It's consensual. Most important, the mediation process keeps the decision-making in your hands. Nothing is forced on you. That gives you the power you need to shape your future.

You can handle things in your own way, at your own pace. This can be especially valuable as you consider what to do with the house. Take your time; get some expert opinions on the value of the property; look at the numbers. Then you can make your decisions in a calm manner, with good counsel and full agreement all around.

Note: If you choose to have your case mediated, you should still work with an attorney to give you legal advice. A mediator is a neutral party, and while that person may be an attorney, he or she cannot give legal advice to either spouse. It is best to hire an attorney who is a proponent of mediation to consult with during your mediation process. Your attorney can even attend the mediation sessions with you.

Collaborative Divorce

Collaborative divorce is a practice that has been gaining momentum in recent years. It employs a team of professionals to help negotiate the best possible resolution for both parties. Recognizing that divorce affects every facet of people's lives, the collaborative approach addresses all of those areas in a comprehensive way. Family law attorney Mark Baer works often with collaborative cases in his Southern California practice. He explains the process: "The collaborative divorce model is basically an interdisciplinary approach where we comprise a team. It's not *husband's team* versus *wife's team*; it's one team." In addition to the attorneys, a collaborative team includes financial experts, child therapists, and a specially trained coach for each spouse. The makeup of the team is determined by the needs of the family members. If there are no children, obviously a child therapist is not necessary.

Like mediation, collaborative is an *interest- and needs-based* process, rather than a rights- and obligations-based process. So if you're determined to squeeze every last concession you can from your spouse, it probably won't work. And if you view your attorney as a surrogate warrior whose role is to inflict pain on your ex, collaborative may not be the right choice. Marriage and family therapist Joyce Tessier serves as a collaborative coach in the greater Los Angeles area. She describes the attitudes that prevent some people from taking advantage of the collaborative process. "Some people have to have other people speak for them," she says. "They get into righteous indignation, and they need to be *right*, rather than married—and that's what brought on the divorce to begin with. And if you need a warrior and you need to win, then litigation is the appropriate process."

On the other hand, collaborative works well for people who can see beyond their present conflict enough to seek a peaceable solution. As Tessier describes, "They not only understand it, but it resonates with the way they live their life anyway." Sometimes, forgiving the other party is an important part of the resolution process. That doesn't mean approving of your ex-spouse's actions—but simply letting go of the bitterness and resentment that they provoked. It's a way of releasing the other party to get on with life. But, more important, it frees you to leave the past behind and move toward your own future.

Implicit in the collaborative model is the understanding that, as vital as attorneys are, they can't address all the issues divorcing couples face. This might seem obvious, but in the emotional crisis of a breakup, people often view their attorneys as saviors and expect results from them that they can't possibly deliver. As Baer notes:

Family law involves many different things: It involves families. It involves the law. It involves emotions. And it involves financial issues. And, there is no training in law school for dealing with emotions . . . We're basically taught that we tell the client, "The court's not designed to deal with your emotions; the court can't give you any kind of benefit or money or compensation for your emotions."

But people still look to their attorneys to resolve emotional issues. "There's an assumption that because we are doing family law that we can deal with this," Baer says. "Well, that's not what we were ever taught." As some experts point out, the emotional component is about 80 percent of a divorce. So trying to get through it without addressing the emotional side is unrealistic. The collaborative approach recognizes that dynamic and provides for it.

Most lawyers also have limited financial expertise. Few are prepared to counsel their clients on the financial challenges they'll face after the divorce is finally over. They aren't necessarily qualified to assess credit damage or help clients rebuild their financial lives. And as we've seen, the complexities of real estate matters are not covered during most law school training. These are the issues that may lie hidden during the heat and emotion of negotiations but that can come back to bite later on.

You'll recall the plight of Sam, our divorced spouse in chapter 2, "Married to the Mortgage." He thought he was in good shape to begin his new life—until he applied for a home loan and the past came crashing in like an unwelcome guest. Working with a collaborative team of specialists can help you anticipate some of these problems and address them while negotiating solutions is still possible.

Also, as we've noted, it's easy to neglect or underestimate the needs of children during a marital breakup. Including a child specialist in the collaborative team can ensure that their welfare remains a top priority.

The *collaborative coach* is typically a trained therapist who functions in a specific, limited capacity during the collaborative divorce process. Joyce Tessier explains: "The coach's role is to focus them on what it is they need to do to come to agreement, so that over time it ultimately ends up in an agreement that turns into a court order." She describes how she might counsel a client in her role as a coach:

> "What is it that you hope for as an outcome, in terms of post-divorce life? This is going to be a small segment of your life, this divorce process. What's it going to look like afterward?" So, you begin right away to focus them on the future. So they get a vision, and sort of a mission about where they want to go.

And as Tessier points out, the freedom of the parties to make their own decisions is always paramount:

> In collaborative or mediated divorces, the decision-making is in the couple, not the professionals. We guide, we help them sort things out, we may offer alternatives, or we may brainstorm about all the ways to come to a decision about whatever they're grappling with at the moment. But ultimately, it's their decision, whereas in litigation with a court trial, or a court-litigated divorce, you go in with a certain set of facts, and then there's

the law that guides the judge in making a court order. And he's not going to know your name when you leave the courtroom, because he's got sixty-three cases on the calendar today.

That stark picture might prompt many to embrace the collaborative model—but they may still balk at the thought of paying not just one, but a whole team of professionals. Yet, when the process functions well, it often ends up saving money for the clients. As Tessier explains:

> When they research processes for divorce, they probably find that litigation costs quite a bit and it takes a long time. Even though there are a number of professionals on a team for a collaborative divorce, it is weighted heavily in the beginning with costs, and then the collaborative professionals drop off as the process proceeds. And they get to a decision sooner, and in the end it costs less.

Having trained psychological counselors present can help break up the logjams that occur when the parties are so hostile that communication breaks down. As Tessier notes:

> When you've got conflict in the beginning, you're not going anywhere with this team until you address the conflicts. Now, what they do is they bring in the coaches first, and start nailing down new ways to communicate with each other and new ways of stepping over the stuff they bring in which is so incendiary for them. And now you've got coaches in the background who are working together to look at *what is it that they need to hear consistently from both of us, so they get the*

message reinforced. When that happens in the beginning, it makes a difference. There's not so much time spent with the full team.

The collaborative structure also includes built-in protection against financial abuse by the team members. The coach, along with the other team members, has a specific role, and "that finishes when the divorce does," Tessier notes. This means that the coach, for example, cannot function as a therapist for the client after the divorce is complete. "Otherwise," she points out, "look at the marketing potential there." And if the process fails, the team members are prohibited from participating in any further efforts with the divorcing spouses, whether the case goes to court or another attempt is made at a collaborative resolution. That prohibition guards against potential conflicts of interest. As Tessier says, "Any one of those professionals could really feather their own nest. So the disqualification is, if this falls out of collaborative for any reason, you have to start over. None of us can participate. And, when it's over, we're not available." One exception is when the agreement contains a clause calling for a review of the terms at a later time. The original team members are allowed to re-enter the process for that purpose.

Choices

There is no magical procedure that can eliminate the pain of a breakup. But there are ways to preserve your assets and prerogatives through the ordeal—as well as your sanity. Mark Baer reflects on the essential difference between litigation and the collaborative model:

> How many people has anyone ever met that ever liked each other, or got along, after they were involved

in a lawsuit with each other? I'm going to say, with very rare exceptions—no one. And yet with family dynamics you're tied together for life. Not until the kids are eighteen—*for life*. Because, absent unusual circumstances, the kids will outlive the parents. Then you're putting them in a dispute resolution process that causes, as a byproduct, conflict."

And that doesn't go away with the judge's final gavel. There are bound to be further negotiations, hearings, and interactions with the ex, as property, custody, and support arrangements need to be revisited. While people may imagine that going to court will end their conflict, they're apt to be sadly surprised. According to Baer, it actually makes it worse. "It won't leave it at the same level," he says. "It increases the level of conflict, because it is an adversarial process."

As Joyce Tessier puts it, "If you're going to get a divorce, the most important decision you can make is *how* you do it—the process." The models described here give you some worthwhile options to consider as you make that decision.

CHAPTER TEN

The Uncooperative Spouse

So far we've discussed specific ways you can manage your divorce and your mortgage obligations. But there will always be some things—and people—that are beyond your control. Exes can be maddeningly unhelpful, just when their cooperation is needed. What should you do when that happens? In this chapter we'll identify the various ways a resentful ex can sabotage your efforts, and how you can prevail anyway.

It's understandable that a partner who didn't want the divorce might resist everything involved with it. The spurned spouse might engage in overtly hostile acts, or adopt a passive-aggressive posture and simply refuse to help in any way. Unfortunately, some also have personality disorders that add an element of danger to the mix. Marriage and family therapist Joyce Tessier describes this type of person:

> You have someone who early in life learned how to respond in a dysfunctional way; they don't know how to behave differently. And ultimately, they drag that around with them: They're not good in relationships, and they have multiple relationships. They are extremely

needy because no one has ever really satisfied what they didn't get a long time ago. They are often people who are self-centered and cannot consider others. So you're talking about the borderline personalities, the narcissistic people.

According to Tessier, these are the people who often keep fighting to the bitter end:

When you get into that kind of extreme behavior that you can actually see that they qualify for those characteristics—those are the ones that wind up going to court, because they don't see the forest for the trees; they're so wounded and caught up in their own stuff.

When they get to court, they may encounter a rude surprise. Judges typically honor agreements between divorcing spouses as long as they seem fair. But if the partners can't agree, the court will decide for them. At that point, uncooperative spouses may find their strategy backfiring.

As we pointed out in chapter 5, "The Emotion Factor," another emotion often lurks behind the belligerent façade that some people display: fear. We saw this most vividly in the case of Kristen and Jim. Kristen pretended to be cooperative, but when it was time to sell she became combative, putting up roadblock after roadblock. That was actually a defensive posture to cover up what she was really feeling. "Most of what happens is fear-driven," Tessier observes. *"What's going to happen to me? What's my life going to look like?"* Whatever the motivation, the resulting behaviors can be exasperating when there are decisions to make and papers to sign. The resistance can manifest in many ways, according to Tessier. You may recognize some of the tactics she describes:

Delay; being argumentative about some small fact; being non-cooperative; ignoring meetings or deadlines. Their expectations are unreasonable in terms of what they can get from it, what they can receive from some kind of agreement; making unreasonable demands for time with the children; or being unavailable for the house to be shown.

That last point illustrates how an ex-partner's passive resistance can foil even the simplest plans. You may have decided to sell the house; your ex may have even agreed. But if he or she is still occupying the home and refuses to let prospective buyers in to see it, you'll have a hard time closing a deal. There may be many situations like this where you need your ex's cooperation—and the former spouse knows it. After the disappointment of losing control in the divorce, your ex may enjoy these fleeting moments of power and exploit them ruthlessly.

That's when it makes sense to enlist the aid of professionals who can mediate for you. After all, that's why you have an attorney—and a real estate agent. As an agent, I'm often appointed by the court to represent both spouses in a sale. In these situations, I've learned to treat the parties with equal respect, which has helped to defuse many volatile conflicts. I can provide a listening ear and acknowledge each party's grievances while offering practical ways to break the deadlock. When there's an impasse, the presence of a neutral third party is essential. In the case of my combative client Kristen, who was obstructing her own sale with a barrage of petty demands, I said, "Kristen, I understand you have a number of concerns, and at this point I think we should make a counteroffer. Here's what I would suggest . . ." I then proposed an offer that advanced her interests while not haggling over every little item. She saw the wisdom of this broader approach, and we were able to move the process forward. The bottom line: When you can't gain the cooperation of your ex, let others take on the task. With the right approach, professional expertise, and objective posture, they'll have a better chance at succeeding.

Along with the tactics we've noted, there are many ways an ex-partner can sabotage your efforts. The remainder of this chapter will discuss some of them.

"I'm Not Selling!"

You may actually decide to sell your property without the consent of your spouse. Some real estate agents will even take your listing on this basis, requiring only one signature on the agreement. But when it comes time to accept an offer, you'll need signatures from everyone whose name appears on the grant deed. If that includes a spouse who refuses to sign off on the sale, the transaction cannot close. This is why I won't take a listing in a family law case with only one signature when both spouses are on title, unless there are extenuating circumstances. And I don't advise anyone to do so; it's a setup for disappointment. If one party refuses to sign a listing agreement, that's an indication that they're not cooperating generally. And it's wishful thinking to imagine that they'll become more agreeable as time goes by. If they're not cooperative at the beginning, they aren't likely to be at the end. Actually, they have less incentive then; knowing that the sale can't close without their consent, they're suddenly in a position of power. In these cases, the worst possible scenario would be to go through the time and effort of marketing the house, and then receive a viable offer—only to find out that it's impossible to complete the sale.

This underscores how important it is to find out early whose names are on the various documents pertaining to the house. As we've pointed out, many homeowners think they know, or at least have a vague idea. But when they examine the actual paperwork they're sometimes surprised. There are so many documents involved in a real estate transaction that it can be hard to keep track of them all. Beyond those connected with the sale itself, there is the *note*, or loan agreement; the *mortgage*, or trust deed offering the house as collateral, and the *grant deed*, which identifies the owner(s). If your name is the only one that appears on the grant deed, you have the right to solely transfer title through a sale—unless the court takes control of the community assets. If your spouse's name is there too, you can't transfer title without the other partner's signature.

Of course, all of that changes when the court steps in. When a judge makes the decision, it may or may not go the way you had hoped. But at least your ex won't be able throw a wrench in the works without incurring the wrath of the court.

"I'm Not Signing!"

You may both have agreed to sell, but when it comes time to sign documents, your ex simply refuses. This is the moment of truth, when the other partner's true feelings may finally emerge. He may not *really* want to see you move on with your life; she may want to hang on to the home for the security it represents. And so the foot-dragging begins.

This can happen in the beginning of the selling process at the listing agreement stage, as we've discussed. It can happen when an offer comes in and you're ready to sign a contract; this can have a long-term impact, because most offers expire within a few days (often seventy-two hours). It can also happen at the end of the whole process when the property transfer is about to happen. It's unfortunate at any time, but it's worst when a deal is in place and the final settlement papers are awaiting signatures. At that point, more lives are affected than just your own. That buyer is a real person, who has deposited money and made plans based on the deal you've agreed to. Beyond that, the buyer's agent, *your* agent, the title and escrow officers, and the loan officer have all expended effort and time to make the transaction work. It's not fair to put them through that without a solid commitment from all the parties. If your ex does balk at the last minute, your real estate agent may be able to convince the buyer to extend the settlement period while you work things out. But if that fails, the sale could collapse.

If it's a court-ordered sale, the ex-partner's stalling tactics won't work. A spouse who refuses to obey a court order risks being cited for contempt. In such cases the real estate agent or spouse's attorney may be able to step in and convince them that it's in their interest to cooperate. But if *that* fails, the uncooperative ones may find themselves fighting a losing battle. The agent or opposing attorney can request the court's intervention in an *ex parte* motion. This means that if the judge agrees, the court clerk will then sign *on behalf of* the absent party, and the sale moves forward anyway. In my role as an appointee of the court, I've completed sales without the signature of a spouse. This demonstrates again just how complete the court's jurisdiction is, which some people find out too late.

"I'm Not Here!"

We've already mentioned the phenomenon of the *disappearing spouse,* in which one party literally drops out of sight and stops communicating. This often happens at critical moments, such as when the settlement documents are awaiting signatures or when the buyer needs to take a final walk-through. The motive for this behavior may be despair, fear, depression, or sheer revenge; whatever the reason, it makes it hard to get things done. Patience and persistence are helpful in overcoming this challenge, but they may not be enough when there are hard deadlines looming—such as a close-of-escrow date or the expiration of a loan approval.

"I'm Not Leaving!"

Sometimes the in-spouse simply refuses to vacate the property. The out-spouse may have allowed the ex to stay as an act of compassion, only to see the arrangement become permanent by default. When that happens the court may assert control and order an eviction, and the process can be swift and brutal. Normal eviction proceedings between a tenant and landlord require a series of legal steps, which may allow the occupants to remain in the property for weeks or months. That's not always the case when a family court orders an eviction. In California where I practice, as soon as the judge slams the gavel, that decision is immediately enforceable. In the cases I've been involved with, the deadline is typically forty-eight or seventy-two hours. The out-spouse can take the court order, go to the property—perhaps with a sheriff's deputy, change the locks, and it's done. This may take place even before the house is sold, if the in-spouse is impeding the sale of the property or otherwise ignoring the court's rulings. The lesson is: The court will do whatever is necessary to enforce its decisions. It doesn't pay to defy a court order.

"I'm Not Helping!"

Even after the big items are resolved, there are always many other miscellaneous tasks involved in a breakup. If your ex is determined not to help you with those, life can become very difficult. The issue may be as mundane as refusing to return the extra set of car keys—or something more serious and far-reaching. And sometimes the problems arise without warning just when you thought everything was sorted out.

We've described the documentation that's required when you apply for a new loan, especially when there may be undetermined obligations such as child support or mortgage payments. At these times, you'll probably need to ask your ex for twelve months of bank statements to document your financial relationship. And that can pose a problem. Loan officer Denise Fontyn describes a typical scenario:

> Let's say you divorce and you do not get removed off the mortgage, and your ex-husband keeps making the payments; you go your way and he goes his way. And you go to buy again. The problem is, when your lender goes to pull your credit, that mortgage is going to be there. When you have a divorce decree stating that it was awarded to your ex-spouse, we still are going to want to show proof that that person, your ex-spouse, has been making the mortgage payments on his own; [that] you haven't been needed to assist with that. So, why is that a problem? Well, by that time, you hate each other. He's going to tell you, "No, I'm not giving you anything. Too bad! I'm not going to give you my bank account information, or printouts showing that I'm making the

payments." What can you do then? Until he decides to sell or refinance on his own accord, you're stuck.

Very few people can foresee problems like this while they're in the middle of a tumultuous breakup. But working with competent professionals who've been there before can help you avoid such problems by taking the right steps *beforehand.* Again, if your ex-partner won't help, attach yourself to the people who will. The issues you'll be facing are complex and hazardous. Don't try to tackle them alone.

When It Gets Scary

So far we've been discussing behavior that's obnoxious, inconvenient, quarrelsome, and vindictive—which is bad enough. But some ex-spouses have psychological issues that can veer into truly dangerous territory. In those cases you may need to respond quickly with serious countermeasures, such as restraining orders and civil or criminal lawsuits. In extreme circumstances you may need to move to a secure location that's unknown to your ex-partner. Such matters are clearly beyond the scope of this book, but if you feel threatened in any way do not hesitate to seek the counsel of your attorney and, if necessary, law enforcement.

CHAPTER ELEVEN

Getting Untangled

Your divorce is almost done; you're almost there! Hang on, because the ride can still get bumpy. If the emotional aspect of a breakup is traumatic, the practical side can be truly exasperating. Like cleaning out your garage, there's always more there than you realized.

We've touched on the biggest mistake people make in their zeal to sever ties quickly: signing over the deed to the house without resolving the mortgage issue—that is, without selling the property or having the other spouse take out a new loan on it. That's an easy trap to fall into, because quitclaiming a deed is a relatively simple procedure, whereas liquidating a mortgage takes time and effort. But you must still avoid taking the easy route. With all such life-changing choices, it's important to be patient and methodical.

As risky as it is to sign over the house too quickly, there's also risk in remaining on title together—even if you're the one who keeps the property, and even if you're making the house payments yourself. Your ex could be doing things without your knowledge that jeopardize your interests. Many divorced homeowners are surprised to find new liens attached to their property—courtesy of their former partners. These may be caused by irresponsible activity or, as with Brad and Shirley in chapter 5, "The Emotion Factor," sheer vindictiveness. In the worst cases, those lienholders can actually force a foreclosure. You may not have caused the problems, but you'll bear the consequences.

What if your ex, who shares the title with you, declares bankruptcy? Suddenly, your house is an asset under the control of the bankruptcy court. And the court can make decisions regarding the house against your wishes.

You may also be vulnerable if you simply allow your ex to stay in the home without resolving the title and mortgage issues, leaving you responsible for a home you no longer live in. When marriages end, people are often angry, depressed, or some volatile combination of both. Some have been known to trash their own homes out of spite or simple neglect. If you leave the home to your ex, you don't know what may occur after your departure. You could end up as the proud co-owner of a wrecked house.

Judge Martha Bellinger has seen this scenario up close. She is now a licensed mediator with Inland Valley Arbitration and Mediation Services (IVAMS) in Southern California but served for years as a family law judge and commissioner. She recalls a case she presided over involving a professional couple, whom we'll call Tony and Diane. They had a large estate, but behind the façade of success, their home life was wracked by strife, caused largely by Tony's high-conflict personality. By the time Diane filed for divorce, Tony had stopped working but was "more than happy to take any money that she was bringing in," as Bellinger notes. Diane had left their home and was taking steps to sell it, but Tony asked if he could stay in the meantime; he was unemployed, emotionally distraught, and had no place to go. Diane took pity on him and agreed—a critical mistake. She didn't understand the depth of his dysfunction and resentment. "So, just out of hatred and wanting to wreak revenge on her—because the house was going to be sold—he just trashed the place," Bellinger says. "It wasn't just a matter of taking things; he had literally thrown paint on the walls and destroyed several rooms of the house! And what was going to have to be done to bring this house back to a salable position was incredible." It might seem odd that Tony would trash a home that he was part owner of, but people don't always act rationally, especially during such a traumatic period of their lives. Plus, Tony was known to be mentally unstable. As Bellinger notes, "The bottom line is, he's angry, and this house doesn't mean anything to him. And he's willing to sacrifice any amount of equity he might get out of that home to make it worse for her."

Diane's compassion cost her more than she could have imagined. Beyond the trauma and wasted time, she now faced the challenge of selling a distressed property that might be ineligible for financing. That meant seeking a cash buyer—who would likely expect a below-market deal. In the meantime she was still responsible for the mortgage payments. The costs of impulsive decisions can be high indeed!

In light of all these unpleasant possibilities, the wise course is to dissolve the joint ownership of the property—but only after carefully examining all the factors, especially the mortgage liabilities. These issues are complex; as we've noted, lawyers and even judges often don't fully understand them. That's why it's imperative to seek the help of experts who deal with such matters every day. And the old saying holds true: An ounce of prevention is worth a pound of cure.

Starting Early

As we've discussed, when a divorce petition is filed, the court assumes broad jurisdiction over all the assets that might affect the final settlement. Often an automatic temporary restraining order is issued on these assets, preventing any movement without the approval of the court. That makes it all the more sensible to reach agreements as early as possible—ideally, before the case is filed with the court. If you can produce signed agreements during the process, the court will often approve them. But once the case is filed, make sure to seek your attorney's counsel regarding any changes you might be contemplating.

Rather than ordering the liquidation of assets, the court will often require both spouses to sign *hold harmless* agreements, basically excusing each other from liability in the handling of those assets. That means you waive your right to legal action if your ex runs up the credit card balance or drains the bank account. Needless to say, you should approach any such agreement very cautiously.

Presuming you have legal authority to do so, the most important action you can take right away is to cancel all active credit accounts that you hold jointly with your ex. How important is this? Loan officer Denise Fontyn stresses it in her advice to divorcing friends and clients. "The very first thing I tell them," she says, "is to call their credit card companies and cancel every joint card they have—immediately."

Credit expert Doug Minor echoes that advice: "Whoever is the primary cardholder needs to remove the other one as the authorized user," he counsels. "On anything that's joint, you want to separate it." Having a joint credit card account with your ex carries similar risks to a jointly held mortgage. You're both on the hook for that obligation, and if the other party is irresponsible or vindictive, it can lead to serious credit harm and financial liability. "The main issue," Minor says, "is you don't want to leave yourself vulnerable to someone else controlling the payments—someone who has the ability to mess up your own credit."

As with all such issues, it's best if you can negotiate this calmly with your ex *before* the divorce is filed, or at least before the court renders a final judgment. Unfortunately, many people confront this topic when the process is already complete or close to it. By then, relations may be so hostile that it's impossible to reach an amicable agreement. The unresolved joint accounts can be like time bombs that explode just when you're trying to rebuild. You may finally feel ready to apply for a new mortgage—only to find that your ex has ruined your credit by defaulting on some joint account. "You do not want to allow that to happen," warns Minor. "You're shooting yourself in the foot."

In some cases you may be able to cancel accounts without the other party's involvement. It depends on the nature of the account and the policy of the credit issuer. If you're the primary cardholder and the other person has been added as an authorized signer, you can probably close the account by yourself. It may also depend on the presence of one little word: Look at the name on your credit account. Does it say *John Smith OR Mary Smith*? Or, is it *John Smith AND Mary Smith*? Denise Fontyn explains the difference, as it relates to closing the account unilaterally: "If it's an *OR* account, you can," she says. "If it's an *AND* account, you can't. *AND* usually means it takes two people, just like in the bank." But even in that case, you may have some options. "If they won't allow you to cancel it," Fontyn says, "you can speak to your creditor and they can freeze it temporarily." That way, she says, "At least the other person cannot rack up additional debt that you could be jointly liable for."

Beyond the debt liability, maintaining joint accounts could expose you to credit damage if your ex defaults on the payments—which is not uncommon among divorcing parties. In summary, when it comes to joint accounts: Negotiate early with your ex-partner, cancel what you can, and try to freeze the activity on any accounts that remain.

Joint bank accounts or investment accounts may not carry the same risks as a credit card, but they should still be liquidated in a way that's fair to both parties as soon it's legally possible. Here is a potential trap that we touched on in chapter 4, "What's Your House Worth, Anyway?" Remember Janet from chapter 4, who kept the house while her ex-husband got the business? That house turned out to be more of a headache than a blessing. Meanwhile, her ex got a functioning business that would provide him with income for years. How was that fair? It wasn't, and poor Janet didn't see it coming. She surrendered something valuable—the business—for something that had little *net* value. That same principle applies to other income-producing assets. It would be foolish to surrender something with real, quantifiable value for a house that's a net loss. But for most of us, it's hard to let go of the notion that the house is an asset worth hanging on to—even when it's not. Denise Fontyn has watched this scenario play out too often. "Sometimes you'll even see a wife or a husband fight to keep a property that is upside down," she notes, "and still give up 50 percent of the retirement account."

The way to avoid this trap is to insist on getting a valuation of the house before agreeing to anything, as we've discussed. Then, request an up-to-date payoff amount from the mortgage company. Subtract the amount owed on *all* loans and liens from the appraised value of the house. If you're considering selling, subtract the sale expenses as well. (Remember, a good Realtor can help you with all of these preliminary steps, typically at no charge.) Compare the net amount with the value of all other assets, and make sure you're getting a fair deal. If the value of the house is negative, as is often the case nowadays, it must be handled like any other liability; the loss should be distributed equally. If you wind up going to court, your lawyer and the judge should be helping you accomplish a fair settlement; but remember, they're not real estate professionals. They may not understand the nuances that could make an arrangement lopsided.

Doug Minor knows the importance of handling these issues early and proactively. As a credit counselor, he often advises clients in the midst of divorce. When they have the foresight to come in early, he's able to help them focus on "how to reduce the damage that's going on, and how to recover their scores in the future." These proactive clients generally fit a profile: They're intelligent, well educated, and successful. That should tell you something! "The other side of the coin," Minor says, "is when I get called by the attorney saying, 'Can you quantify the damages to my client?' And now, one spouse is suing the other." At that point, Minor is serving as an expert witness, either in court or through a deposition. Often, the process has spun out of control and the costs for both parties—financial and emotional—have escalated needlessly.

Are We There Yet?

A common source of frustration is the divorce that drags on for years, essentially stopping both parties in their tracks in the meantime. As we've noted, the sheer duration of the divorce process comes as a surprise to most people. In California where I practice, it's legally possible to finalize a divorce in six months. But it doesn't always work out that way, even when couples don't go to trial. Attorney Pamela Edwards-Swift often has to disabuse new clients of their unrealistic expectations:

> They think that in six months they're going to be divorced, because that's what they hear, and that's what the statute is: You cannot be divorced for at least six months and one day from the date that the respondent is served with the petition. So that's what starts the clock running. But a lot of people think that they're going to be divorced after six months, and that's not the case.

While your divorce is dragging on, you'd probably prefer to be getting on with your life—perhaps even preparing to buy a new home. As always, the challenge then is getting approved for a loan. It is sometimes possible to get financing before a divorce is finalized, but it requires specific conditions. Denise Fontyn explains: "You have to have a signed agreement between both parties and the judge. The divorce does not have to be final, but it has to have been filed with the court. Both parties had to have agreed to it and signed it and filed it with the court." In that light, prolonging the process to settle petty disputes becomes counterproductive. Each day spent haggling is a day you don't move forward—and a day you'll never get back. A contested divorce takes long enough under the best of circumstances. You can shorten that period by focusing on the big, important issues and resolving trivial matters quickly.

If you've gone through a short sale or foreclosure, you may have to wait a while to buy again, but perhaps not as long as you think. With an FHA-insured loan, you can obtain financing right after a short sale—provided you were never late on your mortgage or other bills, and you're not trying to "buy up" or take advantage of a rising market. If you're well situated financially, you can sidestep the credit impact of a short sale by putting off the sale until after you've purchased your new home. This presumes that you have sufficient income to sustain two mortgages at once—rare, but not unheard of. Loan underwriters will scrutinize your debt-to-income ratio considering all your current obligations, plus the one you're seeking to take on.

Things That Can Hang You Up

In chapter 2, "Married to the Mortgage," we told the story of Sam, who couldn't buy a new house because his ex-wife, Doris, had defaulted on their jointly held mortgage. It didn't matter that they'd been divorced for years; what mattered was that his name was still on the loan. Unfortunately, that scenario is very common. But even if the other party stays current on the payments, that shared liability can prevent you from moving on. As we've pointed out, a lender will automatically consider the jointly held loan in your debt-to-income ratio, unless you can prove that it shouldn't be included.

In seeking a new loan, be honest about your income and expenses. Underwriters are very skilled at sniffing out unreported obligations—such as child support. As Denise Fontyn says, "We're no dummies." She goes on:

I'll give you an example: Your 1003 loan application says you have two children, and you're filing [your taxes] single. And I see random deposits into your bank account. Or, vice versa: You have no kids, but your tax return shows you're claiming a dependent. And there are random checks consistently coming out of your bank account. I would ask, "Were you married before? Do you have a copy of your divorce decree? Do you have a child support obligation?" Because I would have to factor that into your ability to qualify.

Trying to sneak something by the loan underwriter won't usually work. Remember, their job is to examine financial documents, and they've seen all the tricks. And what's the number one thing that people try to hide when they apply for financing? "Child support and alimony obligations," according to Denise Fontyn.

Child support can also present problems if you're on the receiving end and seeking a new loan based on income that includes those payments: You'll need to show that you're actually receiving them. As we've noted, just because a court orders someone to make payments doesn't guarantee it will happen. You may need to document your receipt of payments for at least twelve months. And the lender will want to verify that the arrangement is long-term. You may be receiving payments now, but how long will that continue? A lender isn't likely to approve a thirty-year mortgage based on income that's going to end in a year or two. Normally, the lender will need assurance that the payments will continue for at least three years.

Rebuilding

When all is said and done, you want to create an identity for and by yourself, independent of your former spouse. That means establishing your own bank accounts, credit cards, and insurance policies. And yes, it means eventually establishing a new home, which usually entails getting a home mortgage. You may need to do some remedial work on your credit profile to quality for a mortgage with good terms. Credit expert Doug Minor says, "In all my years I've never seen anyone go through a divorce and not have their credit damaged in some way." Rebuilding credit means *getting back on the horse*, to use a familiar metaphor. As Minor observes, "In order to get a good credit score, you have to use credit."

So, how can you obtain credit if your scores are bad? The answers may be much simpler than you imagine. With some basic knowledge of the system, you can begin moving in the right direction. "The thing that people most need to understand," Minor stresses, "is that credit scores are weighted toward *recent information*." In other words, that late payment on your Visa card five years ago may still appear on your credit report—but it's not nearly as important as your payment history over the past six months. That should offer a glimmer of hope: A few positive entries on your report now may outweigh your past transgressions. The same principle applies in deciding which accounts to settle first. Minor directs people to start with the most recently opened accounts. They should "focus on settling those first," he says, "because that's what is most impacting the score."

Then, open credit accounts where you can—making certain

that you don't overuse them and that you pay them in full, on time, every month. If you're having trouble getting approved, start by opening a secured credit card at your local bank, backed up by your own savings account. In most cases, it's quite easy to be approved for these cards since the bank takes on virtually no risk. If you haven't developed the habit of saving money, that should provide a good motivation to start!

If your credit is severely damaged, consider seeking professional help to repair it. There are many credit repair companies to choose from, but you should avoid any that charge upfront fees. Doug Minor, who also owns Easy Credit Relief, Inc., offers another word of caution: "You don't want to start a formal credit repair process until your outstanding debts are settled." There may be old debts that you had forgotten about that are dragging your credit scores down. You can find out by obtaining copies of your credit reports from each of the three major credit bureaus. (Get them for free—once a year—at *mycreditreport.com*.) Those reports will show you which accounts are appearing on your profile. Then you can tackle them one by one.

You may not need to pay off every old debt in full. By the time accounts go to collections status, the creditors are often receptive to partial settlements. They may approach you with settlement offers, or you can start the negotiation process with an offer of your own. Make sure that any agreement includes a *total release of liability* for you. Once those issues are settled, your new financial regimen should be dictated by prudence and commons sense. Minor describes the recipe for sustained financial health: "Diversification, using credit, paying responsibly, giving it time—that's your basic roundup."

Your new, improved credit profile will open up a broad vista of financial opportunities. You'll have the convenience of being able to put certain expenses on credit cards (being careful to pay them off fully each month). You may finally be able to buy a reliable car, eliminating your worry about getting to work every day. But for most people, the ultimate goal of having a good credit profile is to buy a home. Does that seem out of reach right now? Perhaps your previous mortgage is what got you into trouble in the first place. It may have fallen into default during the tumult of your breakup; it may even have been the cause of your divorce. But millions of people have emerged from such disasters to become homeowners again in just a few years. That can happen for you too.

Reaching the Goal

To achieve your goals, you must become your own advocate. Your divorce lawyer is not your savior; he or she is a professional whose task is to represent you in a specific legal action. There are too many elements involved in recovering from a divorce for one person to manage it all. Hopefully, in addition to hiring a lawyer, you'll seek the help of professionals who can help you navigate other areas of your divorce. But how you manage the entire process is up to you. Remember, the best way to avoid disappointment *and* shorten the recovery period is to seek good advice early on. And with the right steps, you'll be back on track before you realize it.

Cheer up—recovery is probably a lot closer than you think!

CHAPTER TWELVE

Landing on Your Feet

*As I walked out the door toward the gate that would lead
to my freedom, I knew if I didn't leave my bitterness and
hatred behind, I'd still be in prison.*

—NELSON MANDELA

Nelson Mandela endured twenty-seven years of imprisonment before becoming a president and world leader. While your ordeal may not be that dramatic, after a difficult marriage and tumultuous divorce process, you may *feel* as if you've been living in a prison. Now, you're ready to walk through that gate into a new life of freedom. It's an exhilarating moment, one that's also challenging. Starting over at this stage of life was never part of your plan. But here you are, facing an uncertain future, as you did when you were entering adulthood—only now you have the scars and wisdom that come with experience.

Will you be able to leave your bitterness and hatred behind as Nelson Mandela did? Doing so will be essential to your success. If you're still seething with resentment toward your ex, you'll have a hard time moving forward. And as we've seen, the desire for revenge can lead to some foolish and self-destructive choices. To use a familiar expression, you could end up cutting off your nose to spite your face. Instead, you can choose to be wise and purposeful in your choices—starting now.

The Power of Forgiveness

The temptation to lash out at your ex—even at the cost of destroying yourself in the process—may be strong. But eventually it will recede, and you'll have the rest of your life to live. Harboring grudges won't help you in that journey. Forgiveness isn't just an abstract notion—it's a key to healthy living. Therapist and collaborative divorce coach Joyce Tessier often helps people grapple with this issue, and she understands why divorcing spouses find it so hard. "You create what is called a grievance story," she explains. "And you tell everybody what a stinker he is or she is. And you keep it alive, and guess what? It's all in your head. You've decided this is the way this marriage runs, or how the world runs. And now you're a victim." Reveling in that emotion may feel good for a while, but it doesn't lead to a happy life. As Tessier asks, "Do you really want to live there?"

She also puts her finger on a question that makes some people balk at the thought of forgiving others: "*If I forgive you, does that mean what you did is okay?*" The answer: Of course not. But clinging to bitterness hurts you far more than it does the other party, and it wastes precious time. As Nelson Mandela is reported to have said, "Harboring resentment is like drinking poison and waiting for it to kill your enemy."

Tessier shares a secret about forgiveness that some people don't realize: "When you forgive, *you* benefit." As she guides her counseling clients through that process, she gives them a vision of hope: "You can feel better, and you can be empowered and not feel so much like a victim." Doesn't that sound like a better way to live? Let go of your grievances. Forgive your ex. As you do, you'll find that you can think more clearly about your life and goals. Instead of reacting emotionally, you'll *act* deliberately, strategically, with the long term in mind.

Author, educator, and licensed mediator Woody Mosten has helped many divorcing couples get through this phase. Here's how he puts it:

> Crisis decisions usually are poor decisions. They get someone out of legal angina in order to stop the bleeding, and sometimes there's nothing left; whereas, real smart people play the long game. They are able to look at different options. They're able to do a strategic plan, look down the road, and make the best decisions for themselves.

There will be a period of rebuilding after your divorce. Use that time to your advantage—it will be over before you know it! Sylvia was a client who went through a period of financial hardship that damaged her credit. Among her other debts, she had literally dozens of medical collection accounts that she couldn't pay. Like many people in distress, she stopped opening her mail so she wouldn't have to face the bad news. Eventually her income recovered, but not her credit. As a result she couldn't take full advantage of her improved financial status. She had wasted the intervening time when she should have been rebuilding her credit profile. She knew the things she should have been doing but habitually put them off, telling herself, *I'll get to it sometime soon.* But she never did. Eventually, when she decided the time was right to purchase a new home, she couldn't—her poor credit made her ineligible for a loan. Sylvia's credit eventually recovered, but she had wasted precious years needlessly.

A Success Story

My friend Seth provides a good example of how to use the lean times wisely. He was a husband and father of two who attained a prominent position in the banking industry—and then lost it all. In quick succession, Seth experienced a contentious divorce, bankruptcy, a foreclosure, and the loss of his business. But he didn't waste a day before beginning the rebuilding process. He approached his recovery with focus, discipline, and an unbeatable attitude. "I'm not the smartest guy in the world," he says, "but I'm very resilient; you can throw me down a number of times and I'll keep standing up." In short order he obtained a secure credit card, then several more. He concentrated on producing an income, any way he could. Within a couple of years, Seth had reestablished his credit, built a new prosperous business, and purchased another home.

There were challenges along the way from several directions. Along with his marriage, his home, his business, and his pride, Seth had also lost his retirement savings. The prospect of starting over in midlife without any cash would be daunting for most people. But Seth didn't dwell on his poverty; he concentrated on his goal. And his eventual success confirmed a truth: *Whatever we focus on tends to expand.*

Meanwhile, as he sought to reenter the business world, Seth discovered that the banking industry, and its technology, had moved on. The computer skills that had helped him succeed years before were now obsolete. With children to take care of, he couldn't afford a moment of self-pity. Seth told himself, "*Okay,*

I have two kids to feed, and I need to get a roof over their heads, and I need to be able to go out into the labor market and establish myself—with a set of skills that I need to develop really rapidly." Seth updated his technical knowledge and was able to offer that to clients along with his decades of experience. Soon his consulting business was taking off. Replenishing his retirement savings was like icing on the cake. "I have a 401(k) and I have a pension," he now says, "which is [worth] approximately thirty-five times more than what I lost."

Seth's positive attitude also allowed him to find help in some unexpected places. He recalls applying to rent an apartment—knowing that he would probably be turned down since his credit was ruined. But the apartment manager turned out to be sympathetic. "Her name was Maria," Seth says. "I remember Maria looking at me and saying, 'Don't worry about it. Just fill out the application; I make the choices.'" To his surprise, Seth got the apartment. "Later on," he recalls, "I found out that Maria had been abandoned by her husband, with two kids to raise." Few things inspire compassion like having walked in someone else's shoes. And such acts of kindness have a way of staying with us. Twelve years later, Seth still runs into Maria from time to time. "She'll give me a big hug," he says. "She's seen my kids grow up—and she remembers; she remembers when I came completely broke, with nothing, and she gave me the apartment." Perhaps sweetest of all, Seth was later able to purchase a high-end home in the very same community where he could barely qualify as a renter a couple of years earlier. "What I realized, coming out of it," he says, "is that, although I'm going to have to make all this effort, I'm going to succeed because *people will work with me.*"

As another wise person put it, "When you set your mind on something you want to do, the world will move to meet you."

Just as important for Seth was his refusal to be categorized: "I never have let anyone define who I am or what I am," he says. He was also willing to let go of his emotional grievances. He looked back at the hurt he had experienced and made a decision that is good advice for anyone facing a breakup, "This is an emotional anchor, an emotional weight, which I don't want to carry around with me. It's done; it's in the past. Let's move on."

Writing Your Own Story

What will your story be like? Eventually the trauma of your divorce will recede, and like my friend Seth, you'll realize that it doesn't have to define you. It's a momentary blip on the radar screen of your life, and you've got better things to look forward to. By taking wise steps now, you can emerge healthy, happy, and ready to embrace the future.

Working with many divorcing men and women through the years, I have come to realize that it's almost always a disorienting time. You will say things you don't mean to say, think things you don't mean to think, do things you don't mean to do, and be someone you are not.

One day, the turbulence will end. The dust will settle. The pain will begin to fade; life will become normal again, albeit a new normal. And though you will forever be shaped by your past, you have the power within to make your future what you want it to be.

One of my favorite things is when past clients come by to see me a few years after they've moved on. Without exception, I hardly recognize them—their faces are free from fear and panic.

And there is a renewed smile, an energy of peace and happiness that fills the room.

They have forgiven. They have forgiven themselves, forgiven their former spouses, and allowed their hate to be set free—up, up, and away from their inner light so they only have room for peaceful energy in their mind, body, and soul. And it shows, inside and out. They focus only on what they can control—themselves. They've let go of the things they cannot control—their exes.

Change begins with you: *Be the change you want to see in the world.*

There is always a silver lining with every cloud. Find yours. It is there.

Godspeed.

About Laurel Starks

Laurel Starks is a divorce real estate specialist and founder of the Divorce Real Estate Institute. Trained in both mediation and collaborative divorce methods, she speaks frequently on real estate and divorce issues to legal and alternative dispute resolution groups.

A former host of the talk radio program Real Estate Matters, Starks also serves as an expert witness in real estate matters related to divorce cases, including the mishandling of procedural aspects therein. She handles the sale of real property in family law cases, and is one of the top producing realtors in the nation. Laurel lives with her husband and two sons in Southern California.

Her website is: www.DivorcingTheHouse.com. She can be contacted for speaking engagements at LStarks@ DivorcingTheHouse.com.

CPSIA information can be obtained
at www.ICGtesting.com
Printed in the USA
LVOW04s0425061215

465580LV00002B/2/P